MW01035362

THE
CONNECTION
Life Transformation Through Yahweh

WILLIAM J. BEAN JR

Stellium Books
Grant Park, Illinois 60940

Cover Design by Annette Munnich
Photos Courtesy of the Author

TABLE OF CONTENTS

THE CONNECTION

FORWARD

I count myself as a very fortunate and blessed man. For the past eight years, I have been able to call Bill Bean my friend and brother. He started as a client and very quickly our relationship evolved to a more personal than professional level.

Over the years I have had talks, conversations, and conferences with Bill and have glimpsed different aspects of the life-events that have made him the man and warrior that he is today. He is a man that is revered, respected, and loved by thousands of people the world over. He has assisted, (nay saved) countless lives and relationships as God has used him as His Spiritual Warrior and Deliverance Minister.

Bill's stories of horrifying events during his early childhood are common knowledge among his followers and friends today. These events that terrorized, traumatized, and produced tragic ends for his mother and father could have, would have, and should have, destroyed anyone. But not Bill. Where Bill's story of a haunting and demonic oppression differs from so many, is that this event strengthened and emboldened Bill to become something more than a mere shell of a man and damaged by-product. It instilled in Bill a need and desire to form a connection with God and with his fellow man.

In "Dark Force" Bill relives his story for us the reader so we can glimpse into the horror that over-shadowed his family.

In "The Connection" Bill stresses the importance of seeking and solidifying a strong connection with God in every aspect of our life. He draws the literal connection between the past events of his life and his present 24/7 Spiritual Warrior life-style… and that connection is God.

Read these pages, not just with an open mind, but an open heart, spirit, and soul. Connect with God and see God do great things in, to, around, and for you and your loved ones.

R. Travis Shortt

Co-Host Mystic Moon Café
Founder Aspyr Communications
Retired Southern Baptist Minister

FORWARD

We come into contact with strangers and people we know almost every day. But how well do we know them? Most of us make snap judgments as if we know the reasons behind their looks, their decisions, their behaviors. But they all have their own story, full of chapters and folded pages, tears, and stains, and we couldn't possibly guess the depths of their personal experiences by glancing at the surface. There is always more than meets the eye, and that does not exclude the simplest of personalities.

When you see Bill Bean or read his writing today, you would never suspect that Bill endured all the pain and hardship he faced throughout most of his life. You will certainly be surprised to hear that he battled depression, that he wasn't close with GOD, or that he was lost without a purpose. You may look at him and assume his life was smooth and effortless. But you'd be shockingly incorrect if you did make that assumption. That is one of the many reasons why Bill can relate so well to the people he helps today.

You'll need to learn the steps in Bill's journey, told in his own words, in order to understand how he made it to where he is now, humbly successful and spreading positivity even in the gloomiest places.

Bill has had a special role in my own life, partially because he is my Uncle Billy, a man I've looked up to ever since I can remember. Even more relevant than that are the stories I heard when I was young. His true encounters spoken around the dinner table, with other family members of ours, confirming every word and nodding in agreement.

Several of my family members grew up with Bill, hanging out with him on a regular basis. While they were playing and getting into trouble without a care in the world, Bill went home to a household that was very unlike the ones he visited with friends. While those friends had witnessed the appalling acts of the dark entities that Bill was forced to live with, they were able to go back to find safety in their own homes. Bill had to stay and coping was far from easy.

Bill still gathers around the dinner table with us but as a new man. Everyone who knew him well growing up is tremendously proud of his accomplishments - the external accomplishments of course, but more importantly, his inner growth. He's a beautiful example of how knowing GOD can save lives, and also that the darkest moments of your life do not define you. Hear Bill's story, and I promise you - you'll learn so much from it.

I was always told that it is better to learn from other people's mistakes so that you don't have to make them yourself. You can instead skip past the pain and consequences, and make better decisions. I don't believe that just applies to mistakes. You can apply the same motto to experiences. Imagine if we all learned from other's experiences? It would be as if we lived many lives in addition to our own short life. It would expand our perception and understanding.

So that next time we see those strangers or loved ones I mentioned above, we see **more**.

Perhaps we would see them the way GOD sees us all.

Stephanie Beaulieu
Bullets of Sanity Blog

THE CONNECTION

THE CONNECTION

THE CONNECTION

ONE
Introduction

Hello and thank you for taking the time to read The Connection. I pray that my story and my triumph over tragedy will serve as a source of inspiration and motivation for you. I'm praying right now that GOD (YAHWEH) will bless every page of this book and may HE bless every word and every letter that I type. May GOD's blessing and favor be on this book and on all who read it. May this be your guidebook for staying super connected to GOD. May it also serve you in the way staying in Faith, Strength and Courage. (Aka Warrior Mode)

I have wanted to write a fourth book for quite some time, but my busy schedule has prevented it. My current life is so much more blessed than it ever was cursed, and I will forever praise GOD for saving me. I'm so far removed from all of the evil and negative garbage that was attached to me that I almost feel like it must have happened to someone else. Never in my wildest imagination did I ever see GOD working through me in this way of becoming a spiritual warrior and a defender of those who are being victimized by evil.

I travel all over America, helping people to become free from a variety of issues. Whether it may be depression, suicidal thoughts or attempts, relationship problems, anger and emotional issues, trauma issues, curses, drug, alcohol and porn addictions, demonic attachment and demonic oppression to demonic possession I have encountered all of it and then some.

GOD surely has worked through me to help people from all walks of life.

It's like being on an endless concert tour, as so many people are in need of my help in some way. I find that it's on the increase, and perhaps it's due to so many things taking place in our world that is leading people away from GOD. I ask that you to put what I have just said to the test by keeping a notebook handy to document every movie, TV show, song, commercial, magazine and or news article that you watch, listen to, or read. Look for blatant displays of evil through symbolism, presentations, song lyrics and any displays thereof. I believe that you will be shocked to find that it's rampant, wide-spread and in plain sight.

There has been a concerted effort over many years to brainwash people into accepting evil and negativity as normal everyday life. I have dedicated many years to these studies, along with studies of human behavior, and it's my feeling that we are in a real crisis situation in America (Especially when it comes to our youth.)

Who's behind all of this and why? I have my opinions, and let me just say that the devil is in the details. Social engineering and the plan to destroy families goes all the way back to the 1950's. GOD has been taken out of everything, and just look at how many families that have been destroyed as a result. The devil does everything in reverse, so he's trying to make good evil and evil good.

Before I go any further, these scriptures are coming into my mind and I must share them with you.

Isaiah 5:20 Woe unto them that call evil good, and good evil
Ecclesiastes 12:1 Remember now thy Creator in the days of thy youth

The only way that we can guide our youth back to GOD is through proper structure and guidelines in the home. The saying "A family that prays together, stays together" is such a true saying. Many colleges, universities, and schools also play a big part in the brainwashing of our kids into not believing in GOD. Their general philosophy is "Do what thou will is the whole of the law." This comes from the wicked teachings of Aleister Crowley, and it directly opposes what Jesus taught us about being selfless.

John 15:13 Greater love hath no man than this, that a man lay down his life for his friends.
Philippians 2:3 in humility, be moved to treat one another as more important than yourself.

That said, I know that we have to love ourselves in order to truly love others. However, there's a fine line between loving ourselves, being humble, caring and selfless, to loving ourselves so much that we become arrogant, totally self-absorbed and selfish. The latter traits are described in the Bible as vanity and haughty. The building up of one's self-importance and self-entitlement can lead to one having no drive or motivation to succeed at anything. Furthermore, it can lead to a lack of regard, empathy, and compassion for others.

The devil is in the details for sure, and he loves every minute of fueling a person's selfishness and lack of compassion. I'll end my commentary with this: If both you and your family decide to truly make GOD first, then abundant blessings will follow. You will not only have a closer bond with GOD, but a closer bond between family members.

TWO
My Journey

This has been quite a journey, to say the least, and it's the greatest thing when you know what your purpose in life is. During my travels, I have helped several high profile people who live in mansions in some of the most exclusive and up-scale communities in the United States. I have been to the homes of many of the middle class as well, and I have also helped people who live in some of the worst places imaginable, places that most would avoid at all costs. I have stated many times that by the power of GOD, I go into places that most people would run out of. Again, it's not my power; it's the power of GOD that is working through me. I have been in many life-threatening situations, including several since I became a pastor. However, GOD is always there and He has protected me from harm each and every time throughout my entire life.

Isaiah 41:10
Do not fear, for I am with you; do not anxiously look about you, for I am your God. I will strengthen you, surely I will help you, surely I will uphold you with My righteous right hand.
Deuteronomy 31:6
Be strong and courageous. Do not be afraid or terrified because of them, for the LORD your God, goes with you; he will never leave you nor forsake you.

My life was full of so much pain and suffering. I was victimized by demonic forces from childhood, and into my adult years. I suffered for many years from major trauma, and I lived in the fear-based, trauma-based mindset. I was also traumatized by horrific physical abuse that was directed towards my mother, by my father.

I was under demonic oppression and I lived in a sea of negativity back then. Both of my parents were dead before the age of fifty, and I have lost many other family members as well. I had no hope, no future, no optimism and no desire to live.

I felt as though I had a black cloud over my head and everything that I did and everything that I touched went wrong. I lived with all of that for so long until I decided to ask GOD to help me. I was so tired of being a prisoner and I either had to get busy living or get busy dying. I chose GOD, therefore I chose life.

I have to take you through the bad times and the sad times, in order for you to have a much clearer understanding of the miraculous transformation that has taken place in my life by the power of GOD.

I have had so many different experiences over my lifetime, and though I wish that I could go back in time and change some, I have a clear understanding that it was all part of my journey to get to where I am now. I look back on some of these things and shake my head and think to myself that GOD surely was keeping me protected in order for me to be where I'm at right now in doing work for HIM.

The first bad experience pertaining to me, (that I was told about) happened after I was born in 1966. Apparently a hospital accident occurred and as a result, one of my toes ended up being severed. The toe was reattached and I still have a circular scar around it to this very day. More of the supernatural events are going to be talked about in the Bean Family Story Synopsis, and now I'll talk about some other things that have happened to me before we get to that.

My Dad had left us in 1975 and he moved to Florida. I was nine years old and very much hated my dad for a variety of reasons during that time. Thank GOD that I was able to forgive him before his untimely death. (He was shot to death in 1987)

He was a good man who made some bad choices in life. His whole being was greatly affected by the demonic forces that had come upon my family and I. As I reflect upon his life, I can't help but feel so sad for him that his life was altered in such a bad way. This man had unlimited potential to do great things in life. He was a rugged and handsome man, and he was blessed with great charisma, along with a smile that could light up a room.

He was a master carpenter and could build a house from the ground up. He and my Uncle Cliff built city blocks full of houses and businesses in Florida in the mid 70's until the mid-80's. He could also tear an engine apart and put it back together. He owned big rigs, painted cars, and did many other things. He was a man's man, very tough, but yet very kind. He became very violent as his journey into alcoholism progressed, and it took him further and further down. He was truly a winner that ended up being robbed of his victory. That said, when we make bad choices, the devil is right there to aid, abed and fuel the situation until it becomes a huge problem.

Speaking of being robbed. I was once robbed at age nine by a man in an alley behind some dumpsters. I had decided to skip school on this particular day, and I recall walking to the nearby Harundale Mall. After spending some time walking around the outside of the mall and thinking about how I was going to pass the time until the school bus showed up that afternoon, I recall walking towards two big green dumpsters on my way back home.

Then I heard a man's voice say "Kid come here." I advanced towards the voice and there was a dirty, scruffy looking guy wearing a green Army coat. He said, "Why aren't you in school?" I put my head down and had no reply for him. He then said, "What is that in your pocket?" I had a white envelope with about twenty-five dollars in it. I had to turn that money into the school for sales of candy. He demanded that I show him what was in my pocket. I pulled out the envelope with the money in it and he snatched it out of my hand and said, "Get out of here." I ran so fast out of there and headed straight home.

So not only did I not go to school that day, I also no longer had the twenty-five dollars to turn into the school for my candy sales. Needless to say, I was in big trouble with my mom. She had to come up with another twenty-five dollars (which was not easy, as we were very poor) and she wanted to know who took the money. I described the man as a dirty looking white guy with brown hair and a green, torn-up Army jacket, with brown corduroy pants and black boots. She called the police and reported it, but they never found the guy.

(Several years later my cousin Mike Zonack and his friend jumped into one of those very same dumpsters to hide from a gunman who was shooting at them. Mike's friend was hit by the gunman and died in that dumpster.)

I've had just about every type of supernatural experience imaginable. From many divine experiences to experiences and battles with the devil and his demons. I have also had encounters with UFOs, Bigfoot, and other non-human looking beings. My conclusion on the matter is that all these phenomena are connected in some way. My body has been pushed to the limit many times over the years, having suffered many broken bones due to sports, fights and freak accidents.

In 1988, I fell from 50 feet into a small pile of road-salt, while working construction on a Maryland state salt dome. I have been stabbed and nearly shot several times as well. I also disarmed a gunman in

2002, while working as a bouncer in a nightclub in the Baltimore area. I have also been a driver and bodyguard, a bar bouncer for 22 years and even had two matches as a professional wrestler. I have appeared in dozens of TV shows and have given over 2000 media interviews worldwide. There's a lot more that I could list here, but you get the idea. My life has truly been an amazing journey for worse and now for the better...
Praise GOD!

THREE
Bean Family Story Synopsis

I don't enjoy writing about these events, however in order for me to show you where I currently am in my life; I must show you where I was. I have stated many times, that in order for me to be where I'm at now in helping others, it was necessary for me to have been there as both a victim and an experiencer. My childhood was truly hellish, and this is why GOD chose me to do the work that I do as a spiritual warrior. I take the suffering of others very seriously and very personally as well.

Bean House 1975

The story you are about to read is painfully true. It chronicles the details of the nightmarish events that unfolded in a house that my family and I resided in from 1970-1980. The three bedroom ranch-style home was located in Glen Burnie, Maryland in a community called Harundale.

The houses in that area were built in the 1940s and were used for military housing. I lived there with my parents William 'Bill' Bean and Patricia 'Pat' Bean, and my siblings are Patti and Bobby.

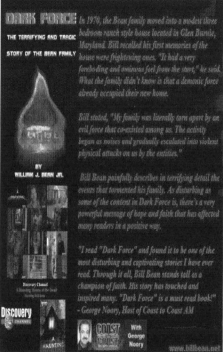

DARK FORCE

THE TERRIFYING AND TRAGIC STORY OF THE BEAN FAMILY

In 1970, the Bean family moved into a modest three bedroom ranch style house located in Glen Burnie, Maryland. Bill recalled his first memories of the house were frightening ones. "It had a very foreboding and ominous feel from the start," he said. What the family didn't know is that a demonic force already occupied their new home.

Bill stated, "My family was literally torn apart by an evil force that co-existed among us. The activity began as noises and gradually escalated into violent physical attacks on us by the entities."

Bill Bean painfully describes in terrifying detail the events that tormented his family. As disturbing as some of the content in Dark Force is, there's a very powerful message of hope and faith that has affected many readers in a positive way.

"I read "Dark Force" and found it to be one of the most disturbing and captivating stories I have ever read. Through it all, Bill Bean stands tall as a champion of faith. His story has touched and inspired many. "Dark Force" is a must read book!" - George Noory, Host of Coast to Coast AM

BY WILLIAM J. BEAN JR.

The Bean family story is one of the most compelling and disturbing supernatural stories on record, as a family of five was destroyed by demonic forces. Long before the Amityville Horror, the Bean family was being supernaturally tormented and divided. The activity began as a feeling of presence and a door slamming shut by itself, which escalated into violent physical demonic attacks on the family members. Some of the experiences include demonic oppression over each family member, Manifestations of black hooded demons along with 4 more human looking entities.

Doors would slam shut, glass was blown out of the back storm door [from the inside] Water faucets would turn on by themselves with such force it would saturate the kitchen and bathroom floors. Foul odors [rotted smells and sulphur smells] would suddenly manifest out of nowhere. There were footsteps heard in the attic and walking down the long hard tiled hallway. Tapping and rapping sounds came from the dark brown paneling on the walls.

The family pets were attacked and tormented as well. Family members were often choked, levitated, thrown, bruised and scratched by the entities.

Discovery Channel featured the story on the 'A Haunting' series and it's one of the highest rated episodes in the history of that series. There's so much more to the story, as it's a true testament that GOD can deliver us from the very worst of things in life.

Original back cover for "Dark Force" (The story was shown on 'A Haunting')

My father, William Bean learned his trade at a very young age from his father Clifford "Pop" Bean, who was a master carpenter. Pop had incredible physical skills and was successful at everything he did. He could build or fix anything, and he passed that right along to his two sons. My father and his older brother Cliff were put to work before the age of ten and were skilled carpenters by their teens. They were also skilled mechanics as well, always fixing vehicles for the family and friends. Both brothers also served in the armed forces for a time.

My mother Patricia 'Pat' Bean was a very attractive blonde with a slender build. She was very kind and charming, and she too had a charisma about her. She was a homemaker and a fantastic one at that. No matter how physically ill, abused or mentally tormented by my dad or demonic forces, she continued to be the best mom in the world to us.

My sister Patti and I recalled the house being very eerie at first glance. The house was semi-dilapidated and had an ominous look and feel about it. A rundown old shed that stood in the backyard was quite foreboding in its own right. All of the windows were broken, and the structure was totally rotted out. It had a heavy, musty smell, and my mother absolutely hated it.

You would enter the house from the front door into a large living room. It had a six foot by six foot plate glass window to the left. Located in between the living room and the dining room, was a built-in bookcase that served as a room divider. Just off of the dining room was a small kitchen. Dad knocked out the closet wall at the beginning of the hallway and converted it into a bar. That hallway had such an eerie feel about it. The walls were lined with dark brown

13

paneling, and there was a hard tile floor that led to the bathroom and bedrooms.

(This picture was taken in 1974. from left to right: Mom-mom Harvey, Patti, and Bobby in front of them, Mom, Dad and me. Look at the large face in the window over my Dad's shoulder.)

I shared the first bedroom on the right with my younger brother. My bed was closest to the door and Bobby's was next to the window. My parents' room was the next one down, and Patti's room was across the hall. Her room was the most frightening room in the house. Looking back on the entire experience, I came to believe it was the main portal for the entities. It was always so cold in that room, even in the summer months.

The first paranormal incident occurred only a few days after we moved into the house. Dad had taken Patti, Bobby and I to visit Pop and Mom-Mom Bean. He did this in order to allow my mother to unpack and organize our belongings without us distracting her. Mom was hard at work unpacking boxes in the living room, when a strange feeling came over her. A sudden chill invaded the living room, even though it was summer. She felt like someone was in the room with her, and she thought that maybe Dad had come back into the house and was trying to sneak up on her to scare her. She quickly spun around expecting to see him, but it shocked her, seeing that no one was there.

Although unnerved and startled, she composed herself enough to continue unpacking. Moments later, she became downright terrified when Patti's bedroom door slammed shut for no apparent reason. Again, she was alone in the house at the time of this incident and after that happened, Mom decided to go outside until we returned. Dad made light of it, saying it was her imagination. However, he knew what she had experienced was real. He always tried to dismiss and downplay things. The truth was that he was not able to control these events, and that drove him into escaping reality.

Dad had his own long list of things that needed to be done as well. First on the list was tearing down the old shed in the backyard. The decaying structure didn't give him much resistance as he busted it apart piece by piece. Next on his list was to put up a large above ground pool. He found a perfect spot on the back side of the house just outside Patti's room. He spent the entire day digging and leveling the base for the pool. The sun was scorching hot, but he was relentless in his efforts to get the pool set up. The next day he installed the liner and the white railing cap.

My father was a perfectionist, due to his apprenticeship under Pop Bean. He was extremely meticulous about his work. He began his inspection, making sure the pool was constructed properly and ready to withstand the gallons and gallons of water it would take to fill it up. As the evening came, dad put the garden hose in the empty pool and let it fill up overnight.

My parents rose early the next morning with eager anticipation of us having our first family pool party. During the night, a portion of the pool had collapsed, and many gallons of water had spilled out into the yard, completely flooding it. After turning the water off, a quick inspection revealed that the pool was, bizarrely enough, pushed in from the outside. The rail cap was bent in with such force that it should have made a tremendous noise when it happened. Strangely, not one of us had heard anything during the night.

Dad fenced in the entire yard, separating the backyard from the large ravine behind it. I heard many stories that a lot of history existed in that ravine and on the grounds of Harundale. The history stems from many Native American tribes frequenting the area. The deep tree-lined ravine stretched a few miles long and had sloping concrete sides for the first half mile. If you advanced farther south in the ravine, it would bring you to a very different looking area. The brush and grass seemed to disappear, replaced by mass quantities of heavy red clay everywhere. It definitely had the look and impression of an Indian burial ground. There weren't many trees there, and the red clay banks jutted out to cliffs in some areas.

In the middle of the night my parents were awakened by sounds coming from the attic. It sounded as if someone was walking or pacing. The attic in that house was very small and nearly impossible for an adult to walk around in. Mom said, "Bill, do you hear that?"

Dad replied, "Maybe its mice." They continued to listen intently for several more minutes when another sound began. It was the sound of the rocking chair in the living room. It had started rocking back and forth on its own. Then they began to hear footsteps coming down the tiled hallway and it sounded like boots or hard-soled shoes hitting the floor with each step. The sounds reverberated off of the paneled walls, as the steps were advancing down the hallway and heading toward their bedroom. Dad jumped out of bed saying, "That's it!" He was ready to confront the intruder, but as he raced into the dark hallway ready for a fight, he found no one there.

Patti was thirteen when we moved in, and she told me that she dreaded being in her room. She always felt like she was being watched and followed in the hallway. Her first encounter with an entity happened in August 1970. It was late into the night and she was asleep in her bed. Something woke her, but she didn't see anyone or anything there. She felt a presence right there with her, and as she was going to get out of bed to get my parents, an invisible entity grabbed her leg. She let out a scream that awakened my parents, and they came rushing into the room to find her curled up in a fetal position. My sister never again felt comfortable in that house. **(She ran away from home in 1973 and married a young man in the neighborhood)**

My first attack in January 1971 was similar to my sister's experience, I was asleep in my bed when I was awakened by something. I felt a presence in the room, but I couldn't see anyone. As fear began to crawl over me, I tried to get out of bed. Suddenly a tremendous force grabbed me by my shoulders, pinning me to the bed. I was flat on my back and totally panicked. I couldn't move any part of my body except for my eyes. I tried to scream out for my parents, but my mouth wouldn't work.

I felt like I was on a carousel at a carnival going around in slow motion. I was so terrified and confused by what was happening to me. Then I heard a tremendous buzzing in my ears as if I had been at a loud concert. Suddenly, as I lay helplessly pinned to the bed, a circular ring of red neon-like light came down out of the ceiling and stopped just above my face. It was very hot and I interpreted it as a "ring of fire." It rotated once around my face counter-clockwise and then went back up through the ceiling.

Only minutes had passed, but it felt like hours to me. I then saw an eerie mist take form, and it was descending from the ceiling. Some people refer to this substance as ectoplasm. To my surprise and amazement, materializing and emerging out of this mist was a beautiful lady, and she was hovering at the foot of my bed. When I saw her I felt an overwhelming rush of peace, love, and compassion from her. She had long blonde hair and a glowing blueish-white gown.

(I have told this story many times over the years, and I cannot accurately describe in words the level of fear and trauma I was feeling at that time.)

Upon seeing her, I noticed that the horrible things that were happening to me had stopped. She was smiling and gazing at me, and I began to calm down. I felt so comforted and protected by her. She remained there for several minutes until I calmed down, then she turned to her left and floated up through the ceiling. The most puzzling aspect of this encounter was that the "Lady" looked exactly like my mother!

(That experience would happen to me many times over the years in that house)

Here's a list of regular occurrences that took place inside of the Harundale house I recall foul odors manifesting out of nowhere and smells of sulfur as well. Tapping and rapping sounds were coming from the walls; doors opened and slammed shut by themselves. My sister's bedroom door would open and shut for many repetitions at a time. Water faucets turned on with such force that it would saturate areas in the kitchen and bathroom. The TV would turn on by itself, and something would turn the heavy channel selector dial. Cabinet doors would open and shut by themselves, walking could be heard in the small attic above us, and footsteps in the hallway were heard often as well. The rocking chair would rock by itself, and a planter rope hanging from the wooden room divider would often swing from side to side as if someone had pushed on it.

Mom and I began hearing chanting in the hallways late at night, along with muffled voices and giggling in the daytime. Sometimes it seemed as though the muffled chanting was coming from inside the walls. We were also physically attacked many times, as were some of our pets over the years. Each and every one of us suffered a form of demonic oppression while living there.

1973 Dad started going to bars after work and staying out most of the night, only to return home in a drunken stupor. The arguments between him and my mother were intensifying, and he began to stay out all night at times. Dad finally confided in Mom-Mom Harvey, telling her that he too was seeing apparitions in the house. Dad described the "Lady," but also described a horribly sinister entity that resembled an undertaker. This manifestation was tall, with chalky white skin, black hair with a black beard and the eyes were black as coal. The sinister image never approached him, but shot foreboding glares at him, which chilled my father to the very bone. I have no doubt that he was under spiritual attack and this led him to escape reality by immersing himself in alcohol abuse.

He began physically abusing my mother on a regular basis from 1973-1975, nearly killing her on several occasions. I have no doubt that he was taken over by demonic forces while under the influence of alcohol. As a young boy, I can recall having to run to a neighbor's house to get the police called on my father. The police responded there regularly during that period of time.

My brother and I saw a tremendous amount of blood-shed in that house.

(When we are under the influence of alcohol and or a drug, our frequency, and vibration is lowered, leaving us wide open for demonic attack. If we keep GOD first and refrain from certain things, we are on high frequency, high vibration.)

Near Fatal Accident 1974... I recall a freakish near fatal incident on a warm summer morning in 1974. Mom's stepfather Earl stopped by our house every morning to deliver bread and other items from the bakery to our family. After a short visit with us, dad and I walked him out to his car. After a brief conversation with dad and a wave goodbye, Pop Earl started up his 1973 Chevy Impala and was preparing to put the vehicle in reverse to back up the street. Dad gave a couple pats on the hood as a farewell, and we were standing directly in front of the car waiting for him to back up.

As we started to move, Pop Earl put the car in reverse gear, but instead, it surged forward. Dad swiftly grabbed me out of its path, and it just missed us by inches. The car then plowed through the fence next door and through a block wall adjacent to the house that served as a barbeque area. Pop Earl was not injured, but he was really shaken up. He kept saying to Dad, "I don't know what the hell happened Bill. I put the car in reverse and it went into drive. When I hit the gas, something was pushing my foot down on the pedal and I couldn't stop it."

He continued to shake his head in disbelief and said again, "I just couldn't stop it. Thank GOD that Billy and you are alright. How in the hell did that happen?"

Lots of Torment and Pestering After getting us off to school in the mornings, my mother's routine was to make all of the beds and then straighten up the house. There were some days that when she returned to the bedrooms, she was shocked to find that the bed covers had been torn apart.

Mom often liked to sit at the dining room table to drink her tea, and there were times that her simple pleasure was interrupted, by Patti's bedroom door inexplicably opening and slamming shut several times, without human assistance. Some days when this happened, Mom would be pushed over her emotional

22

edge and would end up shouting something like, "Stop it, you b*******!"

Mom was always exhausted from lack of sleep, along with the tremendous stress that she was under. She would try to take a nap in the afternoons, on the aged green sofa in the living room. However, on several occasions, the couch would shake violently and it would actually levitate off the floor as she was laying on it. She would have to jump off of the sofa and run out of the house to a neighbor's house until we got home from school.

(I have found that when we take power and authority over demons, they will leave us alone. It's the fear that they feed off of. If we walk in Faith-Strength & Courage=AKA "Warrior Mode," then GOD will have great favor on us and demons will flee our presence. This is due to the power of GOD that is activated within us and upon us.)

In 1975 my Dad had left us and relocated to Florida. I had developed a burning hatred towards him for hurting my mother and for leaving us. After his departure, my mother came under regular physical attack from the entities. She was also in very bad health almost the entire time we lived there. She had developed high blood pressure which led to strokes and eventually kidney failure. She had severe headaches along with kidney pain for quite some time. These ailments along with the unrelenting attacks from demonic forces greatly contributed to the death of my mother.

(She died at the age of forty-four from a Cerebral Hemorrhage.)

Another incident that occurred took place in 1975, shortly before my Dad left us. My brother shared this story with me, as I was not home at the time. I was staying over at Mom-Mom Harvey's that night, but my brother vividly remembers what took place on the night in question. Apparently, my Dad had come home in his usual drunken stupor and as soon as he entered the house, an unseen force picked him up by his throat and threw him into the living room coat closet, breaking the wooden closet doors down.

My Dad was a very strong and stocky built man, and I can't imagine what he was feeling as he was being overpowered in that way. I'm certain that it shook him to his core, and most likely contributed to him delving deeper into his alcoholism.

1976 Window shattering. My brother Bobby was not feeling well and stayed home from school on that day. He was lying down in our bedroom, and mom was ironing clothes in her bedroom. Suddenly, the bathroom sink faucet turned on by itself and water was spraying out of the sink and onto the floor. They both headed for the bathroom to turn it off when suddenly they were startled by the sound of glass shattering. They swiftly moved in the direction of the commotion to find that the glass storm door in the back of the house was completely shattered. Mom was stunned when she realized that the glass had been blown out from the inside. The glass was everywhere, with most of it settling on the back step.

While still standing there still in stunned disbelief, the back bedroom door began opening and shutting furiously. Mom felt like she was going to have a breakdown as she shouted, "Stop it, leave us alone! GOD make it stop!"

Attack from the Undertaker entity. Late one night Mom was awakened by a presence, and she saw the evil Undertaker looking entity standing in the doorway of her bedroom. The sinister entity quickly advanced toward her and began to choke her. She felt the ice cold hands and fingers of the demon as they wrapped tightly around her throat. She thought for certain that she would die at the hands of this thing from hell. After the entity vanished, my mother jumped out of bed gasping for air and ran up the hallway into the kitchen. She needed water, but as she opened the cabinet door to get a glass, an invisible force shot a glass out like a projectile from inside of the cabinet, directly into her face, causing a large gash above her right eyebrow. She was knocked unconscious and had to be taken to the emergency room for stitches and evaluation for concussion.

Mom's stroke and Grandmom Harvey's attack... My mother had suffered a mild stroke in 1976. It happened as she was serving dinner to my brother and me. She looked pale, and was sweating and dazed to the point that she called me Bobby. I knew that something really bad was happening to her, so I called my sister. She came over and got her to the hospital right away. When my mother came home from the hospital, my grandmother came to take care of us. Then one day during her stay with us, Mom-Mom would become the next victim of demonic forces. I recall Mom being in bed and my aunt Joyce (Mom's sister) was in the bedroom with her. I was in the living room with Mom-Mom at the time, sitting on the sofa, and she was seated in the rocking chair. The room was dimly lit and quiet.

We were just sitting there silently collecting our thoughts, when suddenly the chair Mom-Mom was sitting in started violently shaking. Then she was thrown backward in the chair. She had the look of being absolutely terrified, and all of the blood seemed to drain from her face. I jumped up to help her, but I couldn't get her out of the chair. It appeared that she was being held, choked and or suffocated by some unseen force.

Now in a panic myself, I screamed out for my Aunt Joyce and she came running up the hallway to help. Aunt Joyce grabbed Mom-Mom pulling on her with all of her might, finally freeing her from the clutches of the entity and the chair.

1978 Mom had a new man in her life named Richard. Richard was very much like my father. He was a rugged 'man's man.' He was a former boxer and was not afraid of anyone or anything. He loved my mother very much, and he too suffered quite a bit while being there with us. Richard once told me that his impressions of the house were very negative from the very first time he saw it. He said, "I couldn't put my finger on it, but I knew something wasn't right about that house. I never believed in ghosts or that kind of stuff, but that house gave me the creeps right from the start."

Having Richard there with her made Mom feel more safe and secure than she'd felt since Dad left. But not even the presence of Richard would be enough to stop the next attack. He recalled an encounter one night as they lay in bed asleep. They both seemed to wake up at the same time, as it was dark in the room and very cold as well. As Richard gradually became more awake and alert, he began to scan the room, when a terrifying sight caught his eye. By now, Mom was seeing what Richard was seeing too. **(They both became frozen with fear as a large black hooded figure with glowing red eyes was standing at the foot of the bed.)**

He tried to get up and suddenly, they were both helplessly pinned to the bed flat on their backs by the evil force. Richard was a strong man, and he desperately tried to break free, but to no avail. This was the strongest force he had ever been up against, and he was clearly no match for the evil entity. Next, the bed sheet and covers were ripped off of them, and the sheet they were laying on was viciously ripped out from under them. The hooded entity vanished, and the incident ended as quickly as it began.

Another notable incident occurred in June 1979 Mom, Richard, Bobby and I were all together in the living room watching television. Our little poodle Fuzzy was there with us as well. It was early in the evening and Mom made popcorn which we were enjoying. Things were calm in the house. There were no noises or activity of any kind that seemed to be present. It was a very hot and humid night, so mom closed the windows and had put the air conditioner on. We were all enjoying some real family time for a change, and it really felt good to have that once again. However, something would quickly change our night.

We gradually began noticing a foul stench in the room. The air seemed to have gotten thicker, like an indescribable heaviness around us. However, we were trying to remain calm. Then suddenly, Fuzzy jumped up and headed toward the six by six big plate-glass window. He was barking and growling at something that we couldn't see. Then a tremendous force of energy in the form of a small red orb came hurtling through the window. It ripped down the draperies and completely ripped out the two heavy curtain rods that were bolted to the wall. Amazingly, the glass was not broken, despite the tremendous force coming through. Fuzzy never took his eyes off of it, watching it go down the hallway as it disappeared into the closet.

In July 1979, I had a profound talk with my Uncle Clifford Bean. This discussion would change my life and help to shape me into who I am today. My uncle was and is still a devout Christian, and during this discussion he shared with me that if we have strong faith, then we can take power and authority over demonic forces. We can bind and cast them out by the mighty power of YAHWEH in Jesus name. He was doing all of the talking with me nodding my head once in a while. I was taking in everything that he was saying to me, and for once in my life, I felt empowered.

"Son, this is not a game, this is spiritual warfare and the greatest weapon you have is your faith in GOD. I know how young you are, but you are older than your age. You have a maturity that makes you seem older than thirteen. If you feel like this is too much for you, then forget everything I just said to you."

I replied, "No sir, I have faith in GOD, and I'm ready for this."

Little did I know that GOD was preparing me for quite a battle once I returned home.

The Disappearance of Fuzzy It was the Fourth of July 1979, and Richard was taking Mom to a fireworks show at the Inner Harbor. Aunt Joyce met them at the house and went along with them to downtown Baltimore. Mom left Fuzzy in the fenced-in backyard along with Aunt Joyce's dog, a Keeshond named "Shaner." He was a beautiful dog with the look of a Husky breed and was much bigger than Fuzzy. The yard was completely fenced in, and the fence was four feet high. The two dogs had always gotten along well and played together many times. Fuzzy had never gotten out of the yard, and he was far too small to jump the fence. After enjoying an evening of fireworks they returned home, and Mom noticed that all of the lights were out in the house. Even the porch light was out.

Aunt Joyce just wanted to get her dog and leave. She knew that just about anything was possible in that house and wanted no part of it. As they entered, Mom turned the lights back on and everything seemed alright. Aunt Joyce headed right for the back door to call for Shaner. She called for him, but he didn't respond.

She stepped out into the dimly lit backyard to find her dog curled up near the pool. He was trembling and seemed very frightened by something. Mom and Richard had now joined her to see the visibly shaken dog.

Mom said, "Hey, where's Fuzzy?" The dog was not there, and it was as if he had just vanished from the yard. They went out and searched all around the area, but Fuzzy was nowhere to be found. It was now late into the night, and they decided to come back to the house and try to sleep for a few hours before resuming the search. As the morning sunshine crept through the dark bedroom, Richard woke up first. He turned to his left facing Mom, then panic overtook him as he yelled for mom to wake up.

"What the hell! Pat, Pat, get up!" She jumped up saying, "What's wrong?"

As they lay sleeping in the bed, something had placed hunks of curly black hair around her. The hair was placed around her upper body in a semi-circle. They discovered hair under the bed covers, and a trail of it leading from the bed into the hallway. Thick hunks of black hair were in the bathroom and kitchen sinks as well. The hair looked just like Fuzzy's hair and we never saw the dog again...

(Fuzzy 1978)

My first battle against demonic forces... My brother and I had returned home from our visit to Florida, and Mom had informed us about the disappearance of Fuzzy. I recall being hurt by it, but an anger came over me that was more intense than ever before. After arriving home, Mom, Richard and Mom-Mom were waiting for Aunt Joyce and her boyfriend to come over.

Mom wanted to show them the painting of Patti that had been altered. It was a large painting of my sister that my parents had hung on the wall in 1970. Patti was born in 1957 and the painting was done in 1960. It depicted her as a beautiful little girl in a white dress. She looked like a little angel, with her curly locks and bright smile. However, Mom noticed one day that it had been drastically altered. The painting seemed to have come to life and the eyes looked evil. The mouth had a demonic look as well, with an evil sneer. Mom took the painting down and put it in her bedroom closet.

Shortly after their arrival, my mother went down the hall and into her bedroom to get the painting. We suddenly heard a loud crash, and we all went running to Mom and found her on the floor. She had been picked up by the back of her neck by an invisible entity and thrown through the air, landing onto her make-up table and on the floor after that.

Mom was pale white and trembling. Glass was broken from several perfume bottles that were on her make-up table. She had a small cut on her forehead and bright red marks around her neck. Richard and I gently helped her to her feet. She was nearly knocked unconscious, and it took several seconds before she was fully alert. I saw a large bruise forming on her right arm as she continued to tell us what happened.

The thoughts of what happened to Fuzzy, along with the incident that had just occurred with my mother were all too much for me, and I finally snapped. Never mind the fact that I was thirteen at the time, I had had enough of this torment and abuse. I was tired of being a slave to those evil tormentors due to fear. Uncle Cliff's words and instructions were coming back into my mind, and I grabbed a Bible along with the jar of holy water that the priest left for us and all hell was about to break loose!

(We had a priest involved for the last 16 months that we lived there)

I stood alone in the gloomy living room while I yelled out, "I'm calling out the demons in this house. Show yourselves." The five adults became frozen with fear, and none of them said a word. I yelled out again, "In the name of JESUS CHRIST, I command you to show yourselves!"

It was eerily quiet for a few moments, but the battle began with a loud blow on the wall behind the bar. It was the loudest one we had heard so far, and I had no doubt that things were going to quickly escalate. I also noticed that the temperature in the living room had dropped significantly. It was silent for a few minutes until Patti's bedroom door began to open and shut repeatedly. I headed for the hallway and down to where the activity was occurring. The adults cautiously followed behind me, and the slamming door stopped as I approached.

I yelled out again, "I command you to show yourself in the name of Jesus. I bind you foul demons in Jesus name, and I command you to leave now and go to dryer places, In Jesus name." I threw the holy water at the door and then I entered the cold bedroom to repeated my commands. I went into every room saying the same thing, throwing the holy water as the adults silently followed behind me. As we advanced up the hallway into the living room, all of the bedroom doors slammed shut and the house started shaking like an earthquake. Photos, wall decor and paintings fell off the walls, while a foul stench filled the house.

I was not going to be denied in my efforts to battle these evil ones, and I forcefully shouted out, "Show yourselves, foul demons. I command it in Jesus name. SHOW YOURSELVES!" It was like a scene from a Hollywood horror movie, only this was happening for real. I was in the living room, while the rest of them were standing behind me in the dining room. I shouted one last time for the demons to show themselves, and they began to appear in greenish beams of light just a few feet in front of me.

Four entities appeared in those eerie green beams, including the sinister looking Undertaker, the evil red-haired attacker with a long scar down the left side of the face and black eyes. Also the black hooded figure with the red eyes and a female entity that had the look of a witch. She had long, straight, dark hair with sharp facial features and a long black gown. Everyone was in total shock at what had just taken place. We saw them for several seconds before they left.. After they dematerialized, things calmed down in the house. I must admit that actually seeing them manifest together for the first time unnerved me. I was shaking, and the rage that I had along with the adrenaline, was no longer pumping. I felt really drained and wanted to get out of there. We then left and went to Richard's house for the rest of the night.

The Attack on Dallas. This all began, with a 17 year old friend of mine by the name of Bruce. He would have his views about the paranormal forever changed, after the first visit to the house. Bruce, his sister Donna and a few of their friends all worked together at a nearby fast food place, and I visited them quite a bit when they were working. One day Bruce was telling everyone, "Bill claims to have a haunted house."

Donna asked, "Is that true, Billy?"

My reply was "Yeah, it's true."

Bruce said, "I don't believe in that stuff. It's all in your head."

I looked at him squarely in the eyes and said, "Why don't you come and see it for yourself?"

35

Bruce angrily replied, "All right, I'm going to come down there and prove to you that there is no such thing as ghosts."

I asked him, "When?"

His agitated response was, "I get off at ten o'clock, and I'm coming down there to prove my point."

Donna and two other co-workers asked if they could come along, and I said yes. Mom was staying at Richard's house for the weekend and Bobby was staying at Mom-Mom's.

I went back to the restaurant to meet them when they got off work. We arrived at the house around 10:30 PM. Three of the four of them were laughing and joking about the house, but not Donna. She could feel the evil as soon as she looked at the house. She knew that I was telling the truth about our experiences there.

When we entered, nothing seemed out of place. The four of them sat on the sofa, while I sat in the rocking chair. Everyone was quiet, waiting for something to happen. They wanted entertainment, and I wanted to prove that I was telling the truth. About thirty minutes passed and nothing happened. No noises, manifestations, or any of the numerous activities the entities had become infamous for.

The two others present were named John and Dallas. (They not only worked with Donna and Bruce, but they were very good friends of theirs.) John, tired of waiting for something to happen, jumped up and said, "This is a bunch of bullshit. Bruce, you let him con us into coming down here."

Dallas yelled, "Hey ghosts, come out and play." Sure enough, the activity began right after Dallas' challenge. Loud tapping noises began on the walls as if someone was flicking their finger against the paneling. Loud raps were also being heard, like someone taking their fist and pounding the wall. It suddenly got extremely cold in the house, and the looks on their faces were drastically changing into fear. Patti's bedroom door slammed shut and the cabinets and refrigerator doors opened.

John gathered his composure for one final attempt to rationalize all of this. He said, "Alright Bean, who else is here? You have someone else here to scare us, don't you? Is someone in the kitchen? There's somebody in the bedroom too isn't there?"

I shouted at him, "No!"

He decided to go into the kitchen to confront the supposed participant in this perceived charade that he believed I had concocted. John suddenly got a sinking feeling in his stomach as he entered the kitchen, and of course, found no one there. All of the cabinets were gaping open as well as the refrigerator door. But no one was in there that could have opened them. He was now becoming unnerved as he gently and methodically closed all of the doors. He then turned to walk out of the kitchen, and as he did, all of the doors opened again.

He ran for the sofa, white as a sheet, joining the others. These curious, once skeptical young people were now getting a small dose of what my family and I had been enduring for ten years. Bruce looked over at me and said," I'm really sorry that I didn't believe you."

I replied, "That's alright Bruce, but you haven't seen anything yet."

The four apprehensive kids decided they had seen enough and were ready to leave, but Donna had to use the bathroom first. So the five of us joined hands in a chain to escort her down the dark hallway to the bathroom. Dallas was leading the way and had just stepped into the hall when suddenly he was stopped dead in his tracks. An unseen force grabbed him around his throat and lifted him from the floor. He was pinned to the wall, very much like I'd been pinned to my bed so many times, just as Mom and Richard were as well. I will never forget the look of sheer terror on his face as this was happening to him.

Bruce was grabbing at him, trying to pull him down, but the dark force holding him was much too strong. His feet were a good six inches off of the floor. I'm certain that he was regretting ever challenging the entities to "come out and play" as he said it. Finally, after what must have seemed like an eternity, Dallas was released from the entity's grip and dropped to the floor in a crumpled heap. He was semi-coherent, sweating profusely, and shaking very badly. He was gasping for air as we grabbed him and helped him to his feet.

We all raced to the front door in a panic, feeling a sense of relief to be going outside. Bruce was the last one out, and he looked back towards the dining room and saw a black figure, with the glowing red eyes glaring at him. He didn't sleep for three nights after this took place. Many years later he would tell me, "I've never been so scared as I was that night in your house." Dallas, now an EMT, recently told me that he told the guys in the firehouse about it and none of them believed him. That didn't matter to him because he knows it really happened.

The last incident occurred in December 1980. Richard was working overnights at his job and wasn't home yet. Mom slept in our room with us when Richard wasn't there with her. She woke up early on that morning to the smell of burning wires. It was a strong, pungent odor that seemed to be all over the house. She woke us up, and we began to search for the source. We discovered that every electrical appliance was burned up. This disaster ranged from the major appliances such as the television, washer, dryer, refrigerator, to the smaller appliances as well. Later that day, Richard arrived with a truck ready to get us out of that GOD forsaken house. We didn't take much with us, only clothes and personal items. All of the furniture and most of the decor was left behind.

After leaving that house, the story continued and then became devastatingly tragic in the aftermath. We had peace during our stay at Richard's house. It was almost foreign to not be attacked in some way by our demonic tormentors. Though Bobby and I were not having any paranormal issues, my mother was still being attacked on a regular basis.

(When demons are attached to a person, they will follow, no matter where that person goes.)

The stress and pressure from it all, finally took its toll on both my mother and grandmother. Tragedy struck on August 3, 1981, with the death of my beloved grandmother Dora A. Harvey. She died from a sudden series of heart-attacks at the age of 64. I recall being so close to my grandmother, that I called her several times a day and night. I also stayed with her quite often on the weekends, and both she and my Mom were the two closest people to me in my life at the time.

I really can't accurately describe in words how I felt after being told that she had passed. I was zombie-like in one sense **(a very familiar coping mechanism from all of the years of torment and abuse)** and broken-hearted, devastated and numb in another sense. I didn't show it outwardly, but inwardly, I was destroyed. Mom was feeling pretty much the same as me, as she was every bit as close to her mother as I was. My grandmother was her strongest supporter and with her mother suddenly gone, she felt very alone.

I noticed a strange pattern that was developing with Mom. She was asking me to go with her to see old friends that she hadn't seen in quite a while. It seemed urgent to her, and I couldn't understand it at the time.

Then in late September 1981, Mom had suffered a cerebral hemorrhage , which had her on life support and left her comatose most of the time. This took place a little more than a month and a half after the death of my grandmother. There are no words to describe how I was feeling at the time. **(My worst nightmare and a horrible premonition were actually coming true.)**

I feel so bad for my brother Bobby because he was so young, and also for my sister Patti who had to make the most difficult decision of her life. She was the adult out of the three of us, and it had to be her consent to end the life-support for mom. Not long after, Patti was urged by the doctors to stop the life support. My beloved mother Patricia D. Bean died on October 5, 1981, at the age of 44.

I was in such a state of utter shock that I felt devoid of any emotion. I was truly a human zombie for several weeks after mom's death.

I praise GOD for helping me to be able to even function. I also thank my friends as well because they were there with me through it all.

(It's very important to have a support system, especially in times of crisis)

Now I will share the horrible premonition that I had. It took place about six months before their deaths. I was staying at my grandmother's one night when I was awakened by a very vivid vision of a catastrophe pertaining to both my grandmother and mother. I was so upset and disturbed by it, that I began to talk to GOD and ask HIM to take me instead of them. I remember saying to GOD that I could not bear to be without my mother and grandmother, so please take me instead.

I have learned that everything in life happens for a reason, and even though GOD did not answer my prayer, I was not angry at HIM. I was however very despondent and I really didn't want to live anymore. I had quit school in the 8th grade, lied about my age and went to work for a local construction company. I was an undernourished, skinny kid suddenly working with some very tough men. I was a laborer and it required me to lift and carry ninety-pound buckets of drywall mud, along with very heavy sheets of 5/8 sheetrock.

It was brutal in the beginning, yet it was just what I needed to keep me busy and to keep my mind off of everything. The problem was trying to do the same in my free time. I spent that time playing guitar with my step-grandfather "Pop Earl", hanging out with my friends and then eventually forming a band with a good friend who was a drummer.

I was trying my best to keep myself busy. For the most part, it was working, but there were times that I can recall being so depressed that I would wake up and use the bathroom, then go back into the dark room and sit in silence all day and all night until it was time to go back to bed.

This happened many times over the weeks afterward.

Unfortunately, just as I had seemed to have some stability, pop Earl was diagnosed with liver and stomach cancer and passed away soon-after at the age of 70. I was paying room and board to live there with him, but I could not afford the entire rent by myself, so I moved in with a friend and his family. Things were great there, but I still suffered from severe bouts of depression at times.

It was so terrible that I didn't even want to get out of bed some days.

I stayed with them for a while and then went on to live with my Uncle John and Aunt Anne. I continued to battle depression, and I also drank hard liquor and used drugs. I can tell you this, that we as human beings operate on frequency and vibration, and when we are under the influence of alcohol or a drug, we become wide open for the devil to have his way with us. I grew up on the streets, and I would become very violent while under the influence of alcohol. Then one day I cried out to GOD to take it from me. GOD heard my prayer, answered it, and I have not touched alcohol or drugs in nearly 30 years.

I can never thank GOD and praise HIM enough for taking those urges away from me, and it truly was a miracle.

FOUR
Possession

This next chapter, like the previous one, is very difficult to write about. The reason for me even sharing this with you is to show you how severely affected people can become from demonic forces. This is why it's so super important to keep your connection with GOD as strong as possible. Because if we are keeping GOD first then HE will keep us in HIS hedge of protection from evil. Furthermore, if we truly walk in faith, strength, and courage **(Warrior Mode)** then GOD will have great favor on us and evil will flee our presence.

In the late 1980's, I was in a relationship with a woman, who was under severe spiritual attack, due to stress and pressure. I vividly recall how and when her stress level became so great that she actually came under demonic possession. Another factor in this was my background and the demons that were attached to me from my childhood. With all of these factors in place, it was a perfect storm for disastrous events to take place and they surely did. When people are suffering severe emotional problems, coupled with physical and or mental trauma, demonic forces will flock to that person like a magnet.

It's the fear that draws them and they will not leave until GOD works through someone to evict them. At that point in my life, I was not on high with GOD, and I was not on the path that I am now in

45

helping others. I was very much a product of my environment and making GOD first on the mean streets of Baltimore was not high on the list of daily survival.

The possession took place late on a Saturday night, early Sunday morning. We were lying in bed talking and watching television. We paused our conversation for a couple of minutes as our attention was on the program we were watching. I looked over to her to say something, and she was suddenly in a deep sleep. It looked and felt so strange to me because we were wide awake and talking and that fast she seemed to be in a very deep sleep. The room was dark with the exception of the light coming from the television. I watched for a little while longer and decided to turn it off and go to sleep as well.

The room became very dark, and I recall having a very uncomfortable feeling as I was trying to go to sleep. I kept opening my eyes, looking for something that I felt was among us. As my eyes became adjusted to the dark, my fears were confirmed. The feeling was an all too familiar feeling that I'd had many times in my life. As I once again opened my eyes, I was startled to see a black figure standing in the doorway. I remember saying, "Oh no, not again." Then I began to pray and ask GOD to take this demonic entity away.

When I had finished praying it had vanished, but a few seconds later I would hear a sound that I would never want to hear again.

(I have since heard this sound inside of other people that I have performed exorcism's on)

The sound was coming from inside of her and it sounded like a rattlesnake! It was quite unnerving, to say the least. I tried to wake her, but she wouldn't budge.

Then all of the sudden she sat up in bed, very robotic and turned to her left with her head facing me. She swiftly reached out and ripped my cross off from my neck. I turned on the bedroom light to see a hideous sight. The whites of her eyes had turned black. She got out of bed and pushed past me.

She looked at me, and a deep male voice spoke from her and said, "For a man with such faith in your GOD, you surely don't know the Bible." The demon was right; I didn't know any of the scriptures because I had no Christian structure or upbringing. I was never even baptized. I had never more than skimmed over the Bible at that point in my life.

GOD was keeping me strong on the outside, but Inside I felt my knees buckling, and I was terrified on the inside. I shouted, "In the name of Jesus, I bind you foul demon and command you to leave her and go to dryer places." With that, an unseen force began ramming her head into her own clinched right fist for many repetitions. It was an awful thing to watch and I shouted again, "I bind you foul demon in the name of Jesus Christ. I command you to go to dryer places." It seemed to weaken the demon, but it was still hanging on to her.

She was standing in the doorway at this point, and I went over to the phone to call my friend Lenny. It was probably well after 2am at this point, and as I dialed Lenny's number, the demon spoke to me again saying with an evil grin on the woman's face, "He won't answer." His phone rang about 20 times, and he didn't answer.

The demon spoke to me again and said, "Why don't you just give up and join us." My reply was, "Who are you?" It said a name that I will not write in this or any account of this story that I ever give. I have since learned as a spiritual warrior that we do not have a dialogue with demons. They are liars just like the devil, so how could you trust or believe anything that they would say. The only dialogue that I have with demons are the commands and the power and authority I take over them, by the mighty power and name of YAHWEH in Jesus name.

I reached deep down for one more attempt to banish this demon or demons, as once again I said, "In the name of Jesus Christ, I bind you foul demons and command you to leave this woman at once and go to dryer places in Jesus name." Just as I had finished the command, she walked by me to the bed. It was as if something had released her, and she fell face first on the bed. She was once again in a very deep sleep.

I was able to get through to Lenny this time, and he came right over. I remained upstairs keeping watch over her as she slept. I heard the knock at the door and had to go downstairs to answer it. I opened the door and Lenny had a very concerned look on his face. "What happened?" he said.

As I began telling him about it, a tremendously loud boom came from upstairs. It was like a small explosion. We raced up the stairs to find the bedroom door blown apart. There lying right near the splintered bedroom door was a ten-pound dumbbell that apparently was projected by an unseen force into the closed bedroom door. Amazingly, the victim slept right through this entire episode.

As Lenny surveyed the damage, he noticed that she was still asleep. He turned pale and quickly headed downstairs. We sat at the kitchen table, and I explained everything to him. He grew even more disturbed as I was describing everything to him.

As Lenny and I continued to talk, my girlfriend had suddenly come downstairs, and she was very upset at me. She had bruises and knots on her forehead (from the demon ramming her head into her fist) and she thought that it was me who had struck her. She also saw how the door was destroyed and she wanted answers.

She did not recall anything that had happened, **(This is very common in demonic possession cases, as the demonic forces somehow disconnect the**

victim's mind during possession) and Lenny was so freaked-out that he got up and left without saying a word to either of us. She sat down, and I began to tell her what had happened and she just couldn't believe that such a thing was actually possible. She strongly believed that I would never harm her or cause damage to her home like that, but she just couldn't understand how demonic forces could possess a person and carry out these types of things.

I waited until later that morning to call my Aunt Joyce. She was horrified when I told her about everything that had happened. She called a Catholic Church located in the Baltimore area, and they sent a priest out to the victim's house that Monday evening. Neither of us was Catholic, but we greatly appreciated the help from the church and the priest.**(I will not share the name of the priest in order to protect his privacy.)**

Around 6pm that Monday evening, the priest arrived. I opened the door and there stood a large, husky man, with a gentle and kind voice. I asked him to come in and he sat down with us at the kitchen table. We began to inform him of the events that had taken place when he suddenly was attacked, being flipped over backward in his chair. **(Those chairs were very heavy and stable, with all four legs were firmly planted on the floor)**

He landed on his back, while still seated in the chair. I can tell you that the look on his face was one I'll never forget. It was the same look I saw on my friend Dallas' face back in 1980 when he was attacked by one of the demons in the Harundale house. It was a look of sheer terror.

We rushed over to him and helped him to his feet. His back had to be hurting from the force of hitting the floor. Sweat had beaded up on his forehead, and he excused himself to use the bathroom. He came back downstairs and asked me to come outside with him.

Then he told me what I already knew, that there was definitely an evil presence at work in the house. He said he was going to consult with the leading authority in exorcism in Maryland and was convinced that this would require an exorcism. He gave me a number to reach him and told me to call him anytime, no matter how late it was. He was fully aware of the magnitude of the situation, and I would call him on several occasions before he returned to the house.

The next notable incident took place just a few days later involving several of the victim's family members and friends. The demonic force manifested through her while her mother was reading the bible and she grabbed the bible and tore it to shreds. Then I tried to subdue her and she grabbed me by my throat with one hand and it took every ounce of strength that I had to get that one hand off of me. Keep in mind that I was six- feet- three and weighed two hundred and thirty-five pounds at the time. I was a powerlifter and could bench press 500 pounds during that time-period as well.

It was unfathomable how this beautiful five-foot-three, one hundred and thirty-five pound woman suddenly had this superhuman strength. It wasn't her power; it was the demon(s) that were inside of her. Her mom called 911 and within minutes several police officers and EMT's were at the residence. After quickly assessing the situation, they went into action and it took nine of them to hold her down.

They shot her with a large dose of Morphine and in less than a minute, she was out cold. One of the EMT'S asked to speak to me in private. I recall him saying to me, "I don't think her problem is medical. Have you ever heard of demonic possession?" I went on to tell him about what had been happening, and that we had a priest involved.

I can guarantee you that every police officer and fireman there that night will never forget what they saw and experienced. I'll bet sleep eluded them for a couple of days after that.

The possession lasted for twenty two days and ended in the early morning hours on a Monday. Late that Sunday night, as the demonic forces had manifested inside of her once again. I immediately called the priest. He had already been planning to do the exorcism with the other priest, but my call to him that morning changed their plans.

I consider him to be very courageous in coming right over. He witnessed first-hand and was already attacked once, so I'm sure that he was anticipating quite a battle. He felt so strongly that an exorcism had to be done right there and then, as he feared for all of our safety. I not only witnessed it, but I assisted him in the exorcism.

We joined hands in prayer over her and he said to me, "May GOD be with you."

I replied, "And with you." This further enraged the demons in her, and the voice began to shout threats to him. I will not quote what it was saying, as what I'm telling you is disturbing enough already.

The room was so cold, and at one point, she had actually levitated a few inches above the bed. Each time she was splashed with Holy water, it was as if she were being electrocuted. There was a foul stench in the bedroom along with heaviness in the air that was very similar to the house that I grew up in. After several exhausting hours of a titanic spiritual battle, the demons had departed from her and she was set free by GOD.

I can never thank GOD, and praise GOD enough for freeing her and blessing her!

Again keep in mind, I was not a pastor, spiritual warrior, exorcist or anything like that at the time. That said, what I did have going for me was my faith, even though I was not where I should have been in my relationship with GOD. I still knew that GOD was with me and had favor on me. This would be my second battle with demonic forces before I became a spiritual warrior for GOD, and I'll never forget it. Out of all of the hundreds of cases worldwide that I have been involved in, this was and still ranks as the most severe case of demonic possession that I have been involved in to date.

I'm non-denomination and when I perform a spiritual deliverance, more widely known as exorcism, I do not use the Catholic rite in which priests follow. Though I have a prepared way that I follow, some things that I do or say or pray might vary depending on the situation. I'm totally guided by GOD in this and HIS will be done!**(I have performed exorcism's for people with severe cases of possession over the years)**

Another severe case involved another lady who will remain nameless. I actually had to perform two exorcisms on her within hours of each other. After the first one, she seemed to be okay. I left and went to my hotel for the night. I rarely bring anyone with me on these cases, but this time was an exception. I had brought John, Mike, and his granddaughter Angel along. Later in the night for reasons that were no fault of the victim, the demons came back on her. They were tormenting her so badly, that I was called back to the house. I went back and performed another exorcism over her, and she was once again set free by the power of GOD.

I then advanced throughout the house, binding and casting out any and all demons that might be present. I always ask YAHWEH to send HIS giant warrior angels to come and carry off all demons that may be present. Then I ask HIM to have HIS angels carry off those demons and deposit them back into the pits of hell. I always go through the entire house, including basements, garages, and attics.

I must be sure that all evil is gone, and that the home is blessed, sealed, sanctified, purified, cleansed and made holy before GOD.

The house was very big, and the attic was set-up to be a large bedroom. John was with me when I went up there, and he alerted me to a presence. I walked over to where he was standing and not only did I feel it, but I saw it too. The entity was standing between a metal duct-vent-shaft and a window. I was standing approximately ten feet in front of it and John was to my left. I had my Bible in my right hand, and a shaker of a holy mixture (Oil, water, and salt) in my left hand. I said in a very loud and authoritative voice, "By the mighty power of YAHWEH in Jesus name I bind and rebuke you foul demon, and I command you to depart at once." Then I threw my holy mixture at it.

The demon let out a screeching sound (that I had not heard before or since,) as it departed. It was so loud that it rattled the windows. The demonic entity was a very tall, black figure.

THE CONNECTION

FIVE
The Fall

In 1988, I went to work for a local construction company. The job involved stripping the shingles and the plywood off of a pyramid type of structure that stored road salt for the state of Maryland. My friend Frank and I were standing on a two-by-six board that was supported by metal roof jacks. We were about fifty feet up and the jacks were nailed into the structure for supporting our weight. We had no safety harness or safety lines attached to us, and it was so cold up there that our hands were going numb.

There was a very cold and gusty wind blowing that day, and it was cutting us to shreds. We continued on, and as we pried an eight-foot sheet of plywood from the structure, a strong gust of wind caught it, causing us to lose our balance. I moved inward bracing against a 1x3 piece of the structure, and the piece was rotted, sending me right through it to a perceived certain death. Frank has told the story many times and always says that he thought for sure that I was a dead man on that day.

As I fell through, I recall saying, "Oh No!" It was happening so fast, yet it was like slow motion. I fell into a long, aluminum ladder striking my right side against it. The ladder was angled against the inner structure of the salt dome and when I struck it, I bounced off of it and somehow landed on my rear end in some of the salt. I felt my neck jam into my shoulders on impact, and I don't know how I didn't shatter any of my teeth. My cousin John Harvey, who suffered through a life-threatening accident himself, was also working there with us at the time.

I laid there and the crew came running over to me, telling me to stay down. I was so stunned and so afraid that I was seriously injured that I actually got up. Not only did I get back up, but after about fifteen minutes, I went back up there and finished out the day. My knees were shaking so bad, and my legs were like Jell-O. My whole right side was badly bruised from striking the ladder. I had a headache for several days and nightmares of falling for several weeks afterward. **(I should have looked into being a stuntman after that.)**

I want you to take a moment and think about what I have written. This incident happened exactly as I have described it here, and I got up and walked away from it. I should have been killed or at the very least, seriously injured. I could have stayed down and filed a massive lawsuit against my company for unsafe working conditions, but I didn't. I was just so thankful to be alive and relatively unhurt, that nothing else mattered. I would end up quitting that job because I just couldn't go back up there anymore. I had developed a fear of heights and continued to have nightmares about falling for quite some time.

Looking back on this now, I truly believe that satan was trying to kill me in any way that he could before I could become a spiritual warrior for GOD.

SIX
Life Threatening Experiences In The Bar Business

I had two life-threatening incidents take place in the same month back in January of 2002. The first involved an illegal alien from El Salvador and the second involved a local man with quite a lengthy record. I recall working at the club on a busy Friday night, John was working with me and Walt was off that night. All was going well until a lady approached me, asking for help. She told me that there was a very intoxicated Hispanic man bothering her. I walked her back to her table and she pointed him out. He was still nearby, and I approached him. I asked him to leave the woman alone and he nodded in agreement. I walked away, yet knew that this wasn't over with.

I kept my eye on him, and I just knew that it wouldn't be long before he was back to bothering the same woman again. Sure enough, I was right, and I intercepted him as he was advancing towards her. I told him that it was time to go, and he just stood there as if he didn't hear me or understand me. I put my hand on his shoulder and he tensed up.

I had to restrain him in a half nelson/cross face hold. It's a great hold, and I've used it hundreds of times in my career. The hold protects me from getting hurt and doesn't harm the combatant either. I began to drag him out and suddenly a guy that was with him

59

placed a knife in his right hand. I had my left arm under his chin, and my right arm was under his right arm and behind his head. This made his right arm raise and dangle in the air. When the knife was placed into his hand, he swung down as far as he could just missing my face.

Thank GOD I had the hold cinched in pretty tight. If it hadn't been, the knife blade would have slashed or punctured my face for sure. By this time, one of my security guys named Charlie saw what was taking place and raced towards us. The DJ that night was an off-duty Maryland State Trooper, and he also ran over. I made the mistake of taking him to perpetrator the ground and when I did that, everyone piled on top of us.

The worst thing that can happen when multiple people are involved in a fight is to go to the ground, as only bad things can happen down there. I couldn't breathe, yet I was still holding this guy while another security guy named Charlie wrestled the knife from him. Charlie suffered a major wound in his hand that required 40 stitches to close. The police had arrived and arrested the man. He turned out to be an illegal alien from El Salvador. He ended up spending some time in jail over this, before being deported back to his country.

The second and even more serious incident took place just several weeks after the first. It took place on a slow Wednesday night and several people could have died that night. I was in the back part of the lounge, in the DJ booth talking with my close friend Bob. He was not only a great DJ, but a great friend that I very much enjoyed talking to.

His girlfriend Jenny was often with him, and I actually knew her before I knew Bob. She had the same warm, friendly personality as he did. We would play quiz questions back and forth about rock bands and music, and it was always the highlight of the entire night for me. When you are working seven days and seven nights a week, things become very routine and mundane. Silly things like that break the boredom.

Bob was very funny, witty and highly perceptive. As we continued our discussion, we heard two loud "pops." The music was pretty loud, but the popping noises were even louder. It came from the men's room which was located directly behind us in the DJ booth. I knew that the popping noises were gunshots, so I proceeded to the men's room to investigate. Any other time I would have raced into the bathroom to take action, but this time GOD was slowing everything down.

I quietly approached the door and eased it open. Then about fifteen feet in front of me were two men. One was up against the wall and the other was behind him with a pistol to his head. It looked like it was snowing in there, as white debris was falling out of the ceiling from one of his shots. He fired the other shot into the metal urinal divider, in the direction of the DJ booth.

I could feel the blood leaving my head and rushing downward, as I truly believed that someone was going to die that night. He was too far away from me to rush. I couldn't take the chance of him seeing me and possibly shooting the victim or myself. Another supernatural thing that happened was that the noisy, rusty spring on the bathroom door, that always creaked when opened, did not make a sound when I opened it. They never knew that I was there, yet I still could not chance charging the gunman from a distance of fifteen feet.

Psalm 46:1
God is our refuge and strength, a very present help in trouble.

I eased back out of the bathroom and motioned for a bar-back to call 911. Then I quietly motioned for everyone to clear out as I stood to the right of the bathroom door, praying that the man inside would not be shot. I stood at the door hoping to subdue the gunman as he came out. Moments later, he came out, and I let him take a step past me, and then I made my move. I swept his feet out from under him and pounced on top of him. The pistol was protruding out of his right boot. As the pistol was removed from his boot, a bartender picked it up inside of a towel and carried into the kitchen. I held the man down in a loose choke hold for over ten minutes before the police arrived.

He ended up serving time in prison for the things that took place that night, and I pray that he has straightened his life out since then.

After everything was over with, Bob told me about a strange dream that he had the night before the incident. He had a dream that a gun was fired from the bathroom, and the bullet traveled through the wall and struck him in his back!

Psalm 23

The Lord is my shepherd; I shall not want.

2 He maketh me to lie down in green pastures: he leadeth me beside the still waters.

3 He restoreth my soul: he leadeth me in the paths of righteousness for his name's sake.

4 Yea, though I walk through the valley of the shadow of death, I will fear no evil: for thou art with me; thy rod and thy staff they comfort me.

5 Thou preparest a table before me in the presence of mine enemies: thou anointest my head with oil; my cup runneth over.

6 Surely goodness and mercy shall follow me all the days of my life: and I will dwell in the house of the Lord forever.

SEVEN
Health Scares

I had a couple of health issues in the summer of 2005. They came back to back, and it was a very troubling period for Linda and I. The first problem came when I began having chest pains. I visited our family doctor, and he was concerned about my EKG reading. He referred me to a heart doctor, and I went through a series of tests to determine what was wrong with me. Dr. K and the heart doctor suspected that I had a clogged artery, but the tests revealed that none of my arteries were blocked. I passed all of the testing, but the echocardiogram showed that I had scar tissue on a chamber in my heart.

The scar tissue was most likely a result of the chickenpox I had contracted in 1996. I nearly died from that, as it had gotten on and into just about every part of my body. It was a Job-like experience to say the least, and I begged GOD to kill me. I would never wish that experience on anyone. Meanwhile, the heart doctor told me that I needed more testing and that if the condition grew worse, then It would require open heart surgery. I was shocked and stunned and I was very afraid as well.

During the same period of time, I got a call on my cell phone from Dr. K, telling me that I had another serious problem. The day that he did the EKG on me, he saw a large mole on the right side of my stomach. It had been there for years, and I noticed that it had gotten darker and larger. He did not like the looks of it and did a minor in office surgical procedure to cut it out and off. This was not a simple as he thought it would be because he really had to cut into the area to extract it. He stitched me up and said that he would send the mole off to the lab. He told me not to worry and then the call came!

Dr. K was a good friend of mine but had never called me personally about a medical issue. I knew that something was wrong by the tone of his voice. He said, "Bill the mole came back as pre-cancerous A-typical Melanoma." I was stunned by what he'd just said to me. He said that I would need a surgery called Re-excision to make sure that there was no cancer in that area of my stomach.

So a few days later, the surgeon performed the re-excision. He cut a deep and wide hole into my stomach to make sure that I was cancer free.

Linda and I had so many people praying for me, and I know that GOD heard our prayers because no cancer was found. Praise GOD! We all continued to pray about the scar tissue on my heart, and when I went back for more testing, including another Echo-Cardiogram, the scar tissue was gone.

Not only was the scar tissue totally gone, but I was feeling much better and never had another problem with my heart again.

There's only One way and One source for such healing miracles to have taken place. You see the pattern of every time the devil tried to kill me, GOD stepped in and saved me. How can I not endlessly praise GOD every day of my life! I do and I will forevermore!

After all of those issues took place, GOD has blessed me with great health ever since.
Thank You, Father YAHWEH!

EIGHT
Let's Build Your Faith and Change Your Life!

So that's a summarized story of how bad my life was. It was really the short version, as I could have added much more. However, I made my point and you clearly see that I was living a Job-like existence until I called on GOD and submitted to HIM . You are probably saying to yourself, "How could this guy go through all of those things, and yet be where he is today?" Our glorious GOD does work miracles and as a matter of fact, HE works a miracle for us every day with the gift of life.

I called on GOD and HE heard my prayer and not only did HE save me, but HE transformed my life from victim to victor! If GOD did this for me, HE will do it for anyone that calls on HIM.

I remember one day that I was so sick and tired of being sick and tired. I called on GOD and proclaimed that I was willing to make HIM first. I was also willing to accept HIS son Yahshua Jesus the Christ, knowing that YAHWEH saves through him. Not long after, my wonderful wife Linda and I got baptized together and our whole life changed!

GOD was calling me into ministry and HE was calling me to be a spiritual warrior for HIM. So I had to walk in Faith, Strength, and Courage which equals

"Warrior Mode!" This is not a catchy little saying, I truly live my life in this manner and GOD has blessed me beyond my wildest dreams as a result of it.

In order for there to be a true change, I had to purge all of the garbage that was built up inside of me for so long, and then I had to live differently and think differently. No more could I be in the fear-based, trauma-based way of thinking. Always remember that if GOD is with us and for us, then nothing can stand against us. Furthermore, if we are committed to GOD, then we are committed to excellence, and if we are committed to excellence then that means "We Refuse to Lose."

GOD has the most amazing plan for you

"Am I perfect? Absolutely not, but I try to do the best that I can, and I try to be the best that I can be each and every day of my life. I'm committed to GOD, therefore I committed to excellence. To settle for anything less then is a disservice to GOD and a disservice to ourselves.

I refuse to lose." Bill Bean

May GOD feed your spirit with some of these uplifting scriptures and sayings. Let's begin with my favorite one, which is Psalm 91.

Psalm 91
He that dwelleth in the secret place of the most High shall abide under the shadow of the Almighty.

2 I will say of the Lord, He is my refuge and my fortress: my God; in him will I trust.

3 Surely he shall deliver thee from the snare of the fowler, and from the noisome pestilence.

4 He shall cover thee with his feathers, and under his wings shalt thou trust: his truth shall be thy shield and buckler.

5 Thou shalt not be afraid for the terror by night; nor for the arrow that flieth by day;

6 Nor for the pestilence that walketh in darkness; nor for the destruction that wasteth at noonday.

7 A thousand shall fall at thy side, and ten thousand at thy right hand; but it shall not come nigh thee.

8 Only with thine eyes shalt thou behold and see the reward of the wicked.

9 Because thou hast made the Lord, which is my refuge, even the most High, thy habitation;

10 There shall no evil befall thee, neither shall any plague come nigh thy dwelling.

11 For he shall give his angels charge over thee, to keep thee in all thy ways.

12 They shall bear thee up in their hands, lest thou dash thy foot against a stone.

13 Thou shalt tread upon the lion and adder: the young lion and the dragon shalt thou trample under feet.

14 Because he hath set his love upon me, therefore will I deliver him: I will set him on high, because he hath known my name.

15 He shall call upon me, and I will answer him: I will be with him in trouble; I will deliver him, and honor him.

16 With long life will I satisfy him, and shew him my salvation.

Isaiah 54:17
No weapon formed against you shall prosper

Psalm 145:3 Great is the Lord, and greatly to be praised, and his greatness is unsearchable.

Isaiah 54:10
"For the mountains shall depart, and the hills be removed; but my kindness shall not depart from thee, neither shall the covenant of my peace be removed, saith the LORD that hath mercy on thee."

Joshua 1:9
Have not I commanded thee? Be strong and of a good courage; be not afraid, neither be thou dismayed: for the LORD thy God is with thee whithersoever thou goest.

Psalm 91:2 I will say of the LORD, *He is* my refuge and my fortress: my God; in him will I trust.

Psalm 20:4 May HE give you the desire of your heart and make all your plans succeed.

Proverbs 2:1-5
My son, if you accept my words and store up my commands within you, turning your ear to wisdom and applying your heart to understanding, and if you call out for insight and cry aloud for understanding, and if you look for it as for silver and search for it as for hidden treasure, then you will understand the fear of the LORD and find the knowledge of God

Isaiah 41:10
Do not fear, for I am with you; Do not anxiously look
about you, for I am your God. I will strengthen you,
surely I will help you, Surely I will uphold you with
My righteous right hand.

Psalm 40:16
Let all those that seek thee rejoice and be glad in thee:
let such as love thy salvation say continually, The Lord
be magnified.

Psalm 18:2 The **Lord** is my rock, and my fortress, and
my deliverer; my God, my strength, in whom I will
trust; my buckler, and the horn of my salvation, and
my high tower.

Isaiah 26:4 Trust ye in the LORD forever: For in the
LORD YAHWEH *is* everlasting strength

Isaiah 43:2 When you pass through the waters, I will
be with you; And through the rivers, they will not
overflow you. When you walk through the fire, you
will not be scorched, Nor will the flame burn you.

Jeremiah 17:7 Blessed is the man that trusteth in the
Lord, and whose hope the **Lord** is.

Psalm 18:2
The LORD is my rock and my fortress and my
deliverer, My God, my rock, in whom I take refuge;
My shield and the horn of my salvation, my
stronghold.

Psalm 56:11 In God have I put my trust: I will not be afraid what man can do unto me.

Psalm 62:2 He only is my rock and my salvation; he is my defense I shall not be greatly moved.

Hebrews 11
1 Now faith is the substance of things hoped for, the evidence of things not seen.
2 For by it the elders obtained a good report.
3 Through faith we understand that the worlds were framed by the word of God, so that things which are seen were not made of things which do appear.
4 By faith Abel offered unto God a more excellent sacrifice than Cain, by which he obtained witness that he was righteous, God testifying of his gifts: and by it he being dead yet speaketh.
5 By faith Enoch was translated that he should not see death; and was not found, because God had translated him: for before his translation he had this testimony, that he pleased God.
6 But without faith it is impossible to please him: for he that cometh to God must believe that he is, and that he is a rewarder of them that diligently seek him.

The Serenity Prayer

GOD please grant me with the serenity
to accept the things that I cannot Change
Courage to change the things that I can
and wisdom to know the difference
Living one day at a time
Enjoying one moment at a time

Dear Heavenly Father,
Please help me in this time of pain and overwhelming despair. I turn my eyes to YOU as I seek to find the strength to trust in YOUR faithfulness.
I will quietly wait for your salvation. Father, please show me YOUR compassion and YOUR peace. Help me through this bad time. I believe the promise of YOUR Word to send me mercy each day. Though I can't see past today, I trust YOUR great love will never fail me.

Psalm 3:3 But thou, O Lord, art a shield for me; my glory, and the lifter up of mine head.

Psalm 16:8 I have set the Lord always before me: because he is at my right hand, I shall not be moved.

Psalm 23:4 Yea, though I walk through the valley of the shadow of death, I will fear no evil: for thou art with me; thy rod and thy staff they comfort me.

Psalm 27:1 The Lord is my light and my salvation; whom shall I fear? The Lord is the strength of my life; of whom shall I be afraid?

Psalm 33:20 Our soul waiteth for the Lord: he is our help and our shield.

Psalm 94:19 In the multitude of my thoughts within me thy comforts delight my soul.

Psalm 121:7-8 The Lord shall preserve thee from all evil: he shall preserve thy soul.

The Lord shall preserve thy going out and thy coming in from this time forth, and even for evermore.

Proverbs 3:6 In all thy ways acknowledge him, and he shall direct thy paths.

I'm issuing a challenge to you
I challenge you to make GOD first. I challenge you to make each and every day count.
I challenge you to put aside all differences and work together for the greater good.
I challenge you to be committed to excellence.
I challenge you to go out of your way to be a blessing, and to help others in some way on a regular basis.

Jesus said
John 15:13
Greater love hath no man than this, that a man lay down his life for his friends.
I'm not asking you to lay your life down for somebody, but what I am asking is that you consider helping those who are in need, and acknowledge those men and women who are on the front lines protecting our freedoms.
Let's be pro-active and not reactive.
I challenge you to do random acts of kindness for others on a regular basis.
I challenge you to make the most of the greatest gift ever given to us by our glorious GOD. **The gift of Life!**
May you be up to the challenge and may you be blessed and be a blessing.

NINE
The Connection

Now we have arrived at the most important part of this book, and I'm excited to share this information with you. The best way that I can explain how I came to know this information, is to say that GOD gave it to me. I have been blessed with wisdom and knowledge far beyond anything that I could ever imagine, and it all comes from the power of GOD. I was sincere in wanting to renew my everlasting covenant with GOD and I began reading and then studying the Bible.

I started out with a King James Bible (I have several more of them these days) and when I began reading, it might as well have been written in Chinese. I was having a very hard time understanding the old English, and I was having an even harder time retaining any of the scriptures. It was frustrating me to the point where I was ready to put it down and never pick it up again.

Then I prayed and asked GOD to help me to understand what I was trying to read. Sure enough when I picked it up again the next day, I was having a small breakthrough. Then another idea came into my head. I truly believe that this idea came from GOD in the way of not only reading the scripture, but hearing it too. So I tried it and it worked. What I did was open my bible to Psalm 91, and then put on headphones and listened to the scripture as I was reading it. I was not only taking it in visually, but now audibly as well. It made all of the difference and that's how I learned the scriptures and retained them into memory.

It became my daily and nightly routine to study as much as I could, whenever I could. I was also studying ancient history and ancient religions too. It was quite an undertaking but **"Knowledge is Power, and Power perceived is Power Achieved!"** This was most certainly a new way of life for me because of my lack of education. Remember I told you that I had quit school in the eighth grade. It not only bothered me, but it hindered me to the point of feeling worthless and intellectually inadequate.

Therefore, I felt that I could never be successful at anything. How in the world could I ever have a positive effect in someone's life? I lived my life in that terrible manner for so long, and when one is in that mindset, the devil comes a knocking. I started thinking that since I was doomed and miserable, then maybe I would create miseries for others. **(Misery Loves Company.)**

That's how it was for me back then, but this was a new chapter and a new season in my life, with a clean slate. The closer that I drew to GOD, The more GOD was having favor on me. It's very important that all negativity from the past needs to be purged from your memory and your spirit. Yesterday is dead, yesterday is gone and yesterday is not coming back, so let's focus on today, tomorrow and the next day and onward.

When we are in a strong commitment with GOD, then our connection is strong and we are on high. **(High Frequency, High Vibration)** That means the power of GOD is activated very strongly within us. It also means that life is good and that we are moving forward in life.

James 4:7
"Submit yourselves therefore to God. Resist the devil, and he will flee from you."

So as I continued to spiritually grow, something was still missing, and I could not figure out what it was. I was studying the word of GOD every day, and praying both day and night. So what was missing? I prayed and asked GOD to reveal to me what it was, and I received an answer from HIM in my spirit. GOD has never directly talked to me in HIS voice, but I do receive messages that I believe are from HIM in my head. It's like my voice inside of my head receiving the messages.

HE revealed two things that I needed to change right away. The first mistake that I was making, pertained to not beginning my day with GOD. I was so used to waking up and getting off to work, that I didn't think to begin my day by thanking and praising GOD for the day. We all have busy lives and we seem to be able to fit everything else into our busy life accept for GOD.

I changed my way the next morning when I got out of bed. I got right down on my knees to thank and praise GOD for the day. As I said earlier, life is a gift from GOD and we really should thank HIM for it every day. So I said this, "Father YAHWEH, I thank YOU and praise YOU for this day."

Then I said the Our Father Prayer which is **Matthew chapter 6 and verses 9:13**: Our Father Who art in heaven, hallowed be thy name. Thy kingdom come, thy will be done on earth, as it is done in heaven. Give us this day our daily bread and forgive us of our trespass, as we forgive those who trespass against us, and lead us not into temptation but deliver us from evil. For thine is the kingdom and the power and the glory forevermore.

I thanked GOD once again for the day, and thanked HIM for the food that Linda and I were about to receive. I asked HIM to bless it to our bodies. Then I thanked HIM for every single thing that we take into our bodies in that day and night, asking HIM to please bless those foods to our bodies. Next, I ask GOD to bless my day, Linda's day and our family and friends day. Lastly, I asked HIM to work through me to be a blessing to others.

I concluded the prayer with this: Father I can never thank YOU and praise YOU enough for everything. I fear YOU, I love YOU, I worship YOU and I revere YOU. In Jesus name.

Let me now clarify something in case you are confused. **The name of GOD is YAHWEH and it was listed 6823 times in the bible, yet it was**

replaced with the title of LORD. Jesus Hebrew name is Yahshua, which means YAHWEH saves. YAHWEH saves through Yahshua Jesus.
Jesus said in Matthew 6:9 This is how you should pray!

So Jesus instructed us to pray to GOD, by reciting the Our Father Prayer.

I have followed the same pattern since that morning, and I will always begin my day by thanking and praising GOD for the day. Then I recite the prayers. After I began doing this, I noticed that more and more blessings were coming upon me.

The second thing that I was doing wrong, was not praising GOD through song. I'm a guitarist and I'm self-taught. I began to learn how to play at the age of thirteen, by listening to hard rock bands from the 1960's and the 1970's. Music was such a big part of my life back then. I was totally immersed in hours upon hours of listening, learning and playing my guitar along to those hard rock songs. Once I had developed the callouses on my fingers, then it was all about putting the puzzle pieces together as far as figuring out chords and lead scales. To make a long story short, I became a very skilled guitarist. I began to play in bands and had the ability to become a professional, but it never happened.

Looking back on it now, I totally understand why it didn't happen. It wasn't until I decided to bring up song lyrics on the computer that I realized what I was playing along with. I'm not trying to sway you away from listening to music, but as a man of GOD I have to both inform you and warn you about the dangers of certain music.

I could not believe my eyes when I read through some of those song lyrics. I never really listened to the words because I was always focused on the guitar parts. I played the music of all of the popular hard rock and heavy metal bands of the 60's, 70's and 80's. I knew that those bands were not of GOD, but I didn't know how blatant some of the lyrics were in praising the devil.

I think that I had become so immersed into the music, that I was blinded by what some of the songs were really about.

Music was created in order to praise YAHWEH endlessly. The devil is a created being, and was a beautiful creation until his rebellion and fall.
Ezekiel 28 : 13-14-15
13 Thou hast been in Eden the garden of God; every precious stone was thy covering, the sardius, topaz, and the diamond, the beryl, the onyx, and the jasper, the sapphire, the emerald, and the carbuncle, and gold: the workmanship of thy tabrets and of thy pipes was prepared in thee in the day that thou wast created.
14 Thou art the anointed cherub that covereth; and I have set thee so: thou wast upon the holy mountain of God; thou hast walked up and down in the midst of the stones of fire.

15 Thou wast perfect in thy ways from the day that thou wast created, till iniquity was found in thee.

Isaiah 14:13
"You said in your heart, 'I will ascend to heaven; I will raise my throne above the stars of God; I will sit enthroned on the mount of assembly, on the utmost heights of the sacred mountain."

The devil fell because of his pride and arrogance. That said, his fall and casting out of heaven was inevitable anyway. When GOD created man, HE gave us freewill. I believe that there has to be an adversary to man, in order for there to be a consequence for bad choices. GOD will not force us to worship HIM, so people are free to make a choice.

I made my choice a long time ago, and I pray that you will make the same choice......

The point I'm making is that the devil has hijacked most of the music in order to receive the praise from it. GOD is being robbed of the glory and the devil is receiving it. I don't want you to take my word for this. Please go and do the research for yourself and you will see the truth. It took me a long time to come to this conclusion, because when we like something it's hard to let go of it. Especially if the thing that we like becomes an addiction.

Once I realized that I was participating in the playing of some of these blatantly evil songs, I got on my knees and asked GOD to forgive me. I currently write praise and worship songs to honor GOD. I greatly admire performers such as John Tesh, Paul Wilbur and Jonathan Cain, along with many others who glorify GOD through music.

Remember when I talked about how we as human beings operate on frequency and vibration? When beautiful music is being listened to and or performed, it raises the frequency and vibration levels in the environment. It also raises the frequency and vibration in the people who are taking part in it. Our spirit is being fed, and GOD will lift us up to great heights as a result of this.

The same principle applies to a person or persons taking part in listening to negative music. It lowers the person's frequency and vibration, along with negatively affecting the environment around them. It can also open up dimensional doorways in order for demons to come through. Once that happens, paranormal events will begin to take place. Those affected will develop the life sucks attitude, and some will eventually become a great source of torment for others. I have been involved in many of these types of cases and GOD has worked through me to free people from these kinds of traps.

The devil deals in legal rights, so if he feels that he has a right to be in a person's life he will go to GOD. Then he will present the reason as to why both he and his minions can be there. If a person has made a bad choice (we all have at one time or another) then GOD will allow the devil to be present in that person's life. After that takes place, then it becomes a downward spiral with the devil creating a ton of misery and torment for that person.

GOD wants us to flourish and HE doesn't want to see us hurt or suffering. However, when we make bad choices there's a consequence.

So when I began starting my day with GOD and praising GOD through music, what was once missing in my life, had been filled. The blessings continue to amplify and magnify beyond anything that I could ever imagine. I recall times that I was actually homeless, yet GOD provided me with a place to stay. There were other times that I had to borrow five dollars just so I could get something to eat. I went from having no car, to buying the cheapest, junkiest cars that you could imagine. I recall good friends like John Morris and David Coleman trying to encourage me, but I was totally immersed in negativity.

I lived in some of the worst neighborhoods, and survived in some of the most deplorable conditions. I was a member of the "Life Sucks" club for so long, and it all changed when I decided to make GOD first.

GOD has worked so many miracles for me that I have lost count. GOD makes a way, where there isn't a way, and GOD makes the impossible possible!

It brings me so much joy to share this story with you, because I'm so grateful to GOD for taking me from those utter depths. I'm a living witness and living proof that GOD does work miracles. If GOD would do these miraculous things for me, then surely HE will do it for anyone who calls on HIM.

However, be sure to be sincere because no one can deceive GOD. You must be honest with GOD and honest with yourself. If you are truly looking to change your life then submit to GOD. Remember to fear, love, worship and revere HIM.

It's now time to guide you step by step on your path. Like I said at the beginning of the book, if you follow these steps then your life will greatly improve. When GOD's in it, we can't lose. The first thing to do in making this connection is to get on your knees and submit to GOD.

Heavenly Father, please forgive me for anything that I have ever done to upset YOU. I'm truly sorry and I want to turn to YOU for forgiveness. Please forgive me and please have favor on me. I pledge to make YOU first and I accept Jesus into my heart. My greatest purpose in life is to do YOUR will for the rest of my life. Glory to YOU Father YAHWEH forevermore in Jesus name.

After this is done, you can look forward to beginning the next morning with GOD.

As soon as you open your eyes in the morning, look up and thank GOD for the day. Get out of bed and on your knees to say The Lord's Prayer

Matthew chapter 6 and verses 9:13 : Our Father
Who art in heaven, hallowed be thy name. Thy
kingdom come, thy will be done on earth, as it is done
in heaven. Give us this day our daily bread and forgive
us of our trespass, as we forgive those who trespass
against us, and lead us not into temptation but deliver
us from evil. For thine is the kingdom and the power
and the glory forevermore.

Then thank GOD once again for the day, and
thank HIM for the food that you are about to receive
and ask HIM to bless it to your body. Thank HIM for
every single thing that you take into your body in that
day and night, and ask HIM to please bless those foods
to your body. Next ask GOD to bless your day, and
your family and friends day. Lastly, ask HIM to work
through you to be a blessing to others.

Conclude the prayer with this : Father I can
never thank YOU and praise YOU enough for
everything. I fear YOU, I love YOU, I worship YOU
and I revere YOU. In Jesus name.

**GOD has favor on us when we truly make HIM
first!**

I want you to say this next

Daily Victory Prayer
**Father YAHWEH, I give endless praise to YOU
and by YOUR Mighty Power, and YOUR Mighty
& Holy Name I declare victory in this new day I
have an abundance of YOUR Blessings and I'm**

successful at everything that I do and that I touch I
have an abundance of love, peace, joy, good health
and prosperity and I'm a blessing to others and a
shining example of YOUR Love, Mercy and
Goodness. In Jesus name it is so.

Now This

7 Affirmations
1. I praise GOD for this day
2. I declare victory in this day
3. I declare that no weapon formed against me shall
prosper in this day
4. I declare that everything I do and everything that
I touch will be successful in this day
5. I declare perfect health and prosperity in this
day
6. I declare to be a blessing to others in this day
7. I declare to be the best that I can be in this day

You have just set yourself up for a great and
victorious day, by invoking the power of GOD upon
you. Be sure to pray over every single thing that you
take into your body. From a bottle of water to a stick
of gum. Pray over your lunch and pray over your
dinner as well.

Say this prayer before bed every night :

Spiritual Warfare Prayer
**I thank and praise You Father YAHWEH for all
things, and by YOUR mighty power and in Jesus
name, I ask for YOUR giant warrior angels to**

protect me both day and night, 24 hours a day, 7 days a week for the rest of my life. By YOUR mighty power, In Jesus name, I bind and break the power of satan, all demons, all fallen angels, all unclean spirits, all powers and principalities, curses, hexes, vexes, spells, charms, fetishes, witchcraft, sorcery, magic, voodoo, all mind control, psychic warfare, jinxes, potions, bewitchments, death, destruction, sickness, pain, torment, incantations, chanting, hoodoo, root works, money and success curses and everything else being sent my way or my family & friends way. I cast it out and command it to go to dryer places. YAHWEH rebuke thee in Jesus name!

I'm so thankful to GOD for being the messenger to give you this invaluable information. The next thing that I'm going to share with you is Ten Steps to Victory. If you apply these ten steps along with what I have already shared with you, then there will be no stopping you.

Follow these Ten Steps to Victory!
1. Make GOD First
2. Follow the path and the teachings of Jesus
3. Building Faith
4. Forgiveness
5. Find Your Purpose in Life
6. Use the Power of Positive Thinking
7. Set Goals
8. The Importance of Giving
9. Be Grateful for Everything
10 Walk in Faith-Strength-Courage=Warrior Mode!

TEN
The New Beginning
(The Steps)

Step One
Making GOD First
YAHWEH Elohim

The Name par-excellence for the Creator is Yahweh, found 6,823 times in the Old Testament. Through Israel's deliverance from bondage in Egypt, adoption as a nation,and guidance to the Promised Land, the Creator -Redeemer is especially known by this Name.

The Interpreter's Dictionary, 1962, Vol. 4, page 923, says: Yahweh -The vocalization of the four consonants of the Israelite name for the Creator, which scholars believe to approximate the original pronunciation.

The Encyclopedia Judaica, 1972, Vol. 7, page 680, states emphatically:

The true pronunciation of the Name YHWH was never lost. Several early Greek writers of the Christian Church testify that the Name was pronounced 'YAHWEH'.

Prayer is the counter-punch of pride. The antidote to the passion of hatred. The best rule in

making just laws. A stronghold for peace and a safeguard for travelers. The source of fertility for the farmer. A safe harbor on the storms of this life. The source of all true joy!

Psalm 145:3

Great is the Lord, greatly to be praised. HIS greatness is unsearchable.

Psalm 104:3

HE makes the clouds HIS chariot and HE rides on the wings of the wind.

Step Two
Follow the Path and the teachings of Jesus
Jesus
Yahshua Mashiah

The most important part of Jesus' message is that we are to love GOD with everything in our being.

Matthew 22:37-40 Jesus said unto him, Thou shalt love the Lord thy God with all thy heart, and with all thy soul, and with all thy mind. This is the first and great commandment. And the second is like, unto it, Thou shalt love thy neighbor as thyself. On these two commandments hang all the law and the prophets.
John 3:16 For God so loved the world, that he gave his only begotten Son, that whosoever believe in him should not perish, but have everlasting life.
John 14:6 I am the way, the truth, and the life
Matthew 6:33 But seek ye first the kingdom of God, and his righteousness, and all these things shall be added unto you.

Step Three
Building Faith

Matthew 15:28 Then Jesus answered, "Woman, you have great faith! Your request is granted." And her daughter was healed from that very hour.

Faith is the single most important thing that we have in our walk with GOD. It's by faith that miracles happen, and it's by faith that GOD makes the impossible possible. If we truly trust in GOD to show us the way and to help us in our life, then our connection becomes very strong and abundant blessings will follow.

Living in faith will not make your life perfect, but I can assure you that it will greatly improve it. GOD delights when we choose to come back to HIM in fear, love, worship and reverence. Some might say why fear GOD? I have no fear of anyone or anything, except for the ONE who created me and who holds my very life in HIS hands.

James 1:3 Because the testing of your faith develops your perseverance

Step Four
Forgiveness

When we show hate and unforgiveness for someone, it poisons our spirit and it affects us in many different ways. When we forgive, it is as much for us as it is for the other person. I have done wrong to people and I have offended people in the past. I ask for anyone that I have ever wronged in any way, to forgive me, just as I forgive all who have done wrong to me and offended me.

We must forgive in order to move forward...

Matthew 6:15 But if ye forgive not men their trespasses, neither will your Father forgive your trespasses.

"To Err is human, but to forgive divine"
Alexander Pope

Step Five
Finding Your Purpose

For many years I had no idea what my purpose in life was, nor did I care to know. I had no ambition, no goals and no hope for a future. Again it wasn't until my wife and I decided to make GOD first in our lives, that GOD suddenly revealed my calling.

The feeling would never leave me. I'd wake up in the morning thinking about helping people, and I would go to bed thinking about it as well. I thought to myself that GOD must be making a mistake by calling someone like me to actually go and free others from evil.

Quite to the contrary, as GOD knew exactly what HE was doing in calling me into becoming a spiritual warrior for HIM. As I stated at the beginning of this book, I could not be where I am now as a warrior, had I not been a victim. We can't be a help and a service to someone, unless we have been there to understand what they are going through.

I'm so thankful to GOD for calling me into service to help others. Thank YOU, FATHER, for my calling and my purpose in life, and I wouldn't change it for anything.

The only way to truly know your purpose is to seek GOD and let HIM guide you to it. Everything is in HIS time and if you remain faithful, HE will reveal it to you.

Step Six
The Power of Positive Thinking

If we truly believe that we can do something, then we can do it. The mind is very powerful and works in concert with our body and spirit. The spirit puts the thought in our mind, and the mind transfers the thought to the body. I can surely tell you this, my life changed for the better when my mindset changed.

I used to operate in the negative every day. I would wake up, and expect something to go wrong in that day. Guess what, often times things did go wrong because I manifested it. We can invoke curses on ourselves and on others, by speaking things into existence. This is why it's so important to live in the positive, loving and caring about others.

It goes right back to frequency and vibration. When we are with GOD and walking in faith, we are on high. When we are negative, we are on low. When we are on low, life sucks and it's like the black cloud is over your head. Nothing goes right and there's always a problem, a situation and never an answer.

GOD is life, light, love, hope, faith and all good things. I believe that YAHWEH spoke the world into existence. I also believe that when HE created us, we were made with a part of HIM inside each of us. This would explain why we have power, authority and dominion over the earth, and every living thing. My point is that if GOD did speak the world into existence, then we as HIS creation also have the power to speak things into existence.

Stay on high and keep moving forward in Warrior Mode.

Step Seven
Setting Goals

Many years ago as a teenager, I recall my cousin Phillip saying one of the most profound things to me. We were raking leaves one day and he said, "Outline and define." I certainly wasn't gravitating to what he said while having a rake in my hands, but his words never left me.

As I got older and more mature, I began to understand the meaning of what he said. Every man's life touches another in some way, and we always hope that it's in a good way. We have the power to affect others' lives with words and actions. Phillip had no idea how much those words would help to shape who I am today.

By outlining, we bring the goal and the task before us. By defining, we begin to work on it and shape it in the way that we want it to be. For instance, in writing my books, I have to outline by topic and get the content typed up. Then I begin to shape and define the story in the order that it needs to be.

It's not easy achieving a goal, especially a lofty one. It requires Faith, Strength, Courage, Hard Work, Dedication, Perseverance and long hours. However, if you want something bad enough then you will achieve it. Never give up, and if you get knocked down a thousand times, get back up a thousand and one!

Step Eight
The Importance of Giving

Give with a glad heart and never worry about receiving anything in return. GOD always rewards our kindness and our compassion towards others. Remember it's always better to give than to receive. Jesus was selfless; therefore we should all try to follow his example in helping others. Some of the most gratifying times of my life have come when helping the homeless, special needs people, and of course people under the influence of evil. I recall many kind-hearted gestures from my good friend Mike Suppa, who like me loves to give. Can you imagine how fast our world would change if we all began to reach out in helping others?

My biggest dream is for the barriers that separate us as human beings to come down. We are all GOD's children and should build each other up, not tear each other down. I'm well aware that there are some bad people in this world, with bad intentions. However, there are so many more good people in this world, with good intentions. GOD's light will always engulf the darkness, and the good people of the earth need to always remember that.

Together we can make a positive difference. The devil is the author of division, and this is why we have so much hatred and strife in the world today. There will never be peace as long as we are divided.

United we are strong and divided we fall. The devil knows this better than anyone.

Give with a glad heart and your reward will come from GOD!

Step Nine
Gratitude

Always remember that every day is a gift from GOD, and we are not promised tomorrow. It's very important to thank GOD for each and every day. Let your loved ones know how much you love and appreciate them. If someone helps you in some way, let them know how grateful you are for their help. I'm grateful to GOD for my wonderful life, and for all of HIS abundant blessings.

I tell HIM every day (several times) that I can never thank and praise HIM enough for everything that HE's done, for everything that HE's doing and for everything that HE's going to do for me.

Gratitude balances the attitude!

Psalm 92:1 It is good to give thanks to the LORD And to sing praises to Your name, O Most High;
1 Chronicles 23:30 They are to stand every morning to thank and to praise the LORD, and likewise at evening

Step Ten
Faith-Strength-Courage = Warrior Mode

Well, we have reached the last and certainly not the least step in your declaration of victory. Most of us do not realize that we are in a spiritual battle on a daily basis. Technology is distracting people and dulling their senses. This is all be design in order to lead people away from GOD. The devil is always in the details when it comes to these things, and I want you to be wide awake.

1 Peter 5:8 Be sober and vigilant; because your adversary the devil, is a roaring lion, walking about, seeking whom he may devour:

It ultimately comes down to the choices we make, as satan and his minions can have an influence if we open the door to him. So fill your mind and your spirit with good and positive things. Always be on guard, because the enemy never stops trying to cause problems. If you feel like you are under spiritual attack, then address it ASAP! Say the spiritual warfare prayer right away, and say it every time that you feel that there's a problem. Also remember that if you make a mistake and sin before GOD, get on your knees and confess it before HIM and a blessing will follow.

Hebrews 11:6 But without faith, it is impossible to please him: for he that cometh to God must believe that he is and that he is a rewarder of them that diligently seek him.

Let's break all of the strongholds and all of the legal rights that the devil feels he has over your life. Be sure to address every aspect of your life, as you want a total purging. Also, remember that this can happen to anyone. The devil doesn't have a preference, as he hates all human beings. There's one common thread in all of the cases that I have been involved in. The victims have suffered some type of trauma due to sexual molestation, rape, beatings as well as other atrocities.

The devil and his demons are drawn to a victim from both fear and trauma. It draws them like a magnet because of the low frequency and vibration. I'll even go a step further in that the Pineal and Adrenal Glands produce secretions that are actually used on the black market. These secretions are sold for very large sums of money, and it's been called the most powerful drug on the earth. That drug is called Adrenochrome.

(Adrenochrome is a chemical produced by the human body when adrenaline oxidizes or "hits the air." It's produced when the body is traumatized in some way such as through torture or extreme terror.)

That said, when a person is under demonic attack, and if they have suffered any type of trauma, then it will require me or someone like me, to perform a spiritual deliverance. I would then suggest a baptism after the deliverance. Baptism is the renewal of the covenant, along with the final blessing and purification before GOD. I have baptized many people right in their own bathtubs. It doesn't matter where the body of water is, as long as the water is blessed.

I always bless the water before allowing a person to step into it.

GOD has worked through me to help pastors and their families. I have also helped their congregations at various churches around the country. I always begin the service in prayer. Then I talk about my life and afterward, the people line the aisles for spiritual deliverance. There's no way to describe the feeling I get when GOD has worked through me to free someone and change their life.

If your problems are severe, and you are under heavy demonic attack then don't hesitate to contact me for help. My direct email is beanoffice@yahoo.com My websites are www.billbean.net and www.billbeanministries.com

May this book serve as a guidebook for you and if you follow this advice, watch how quickly your life changes for the better. I'm not telling you that you will become a millionaire or that monetary riches will come as a result of following my advice. **(If that should happen then praise GOD and send a donation to my ministry lol.)** However what surely will come upon you is a richness in the spirit, and a fulfillment that money can't buy.

Always remember that if GOD is with us and for us, then nothing can stand against us.

I want you to get busy living and to get busy winning.

Father YAHWEH I ask that YOU bless the person reading this in every aspect of their life. May YOU free them from the chains that the enemy has built over them. May YOU keep them in YOUR hedge of protection twenty-four hours a day, seven days a week. May YOU loose the blessings of Deuteronomy 28 over them and may YOU bless their going in and coming out, and may YOU make their enemies to flee from them in seven different directions. May YOU bless them with an abundance of love, peace, joy, good health and prosperity for life.

May YOU work through them to be a blessing to others and a shining example of YOUR love, mercy and goodness.

I declare this by YOUR mighty power and YOUR mighty and holy name in Jesus name! **Thank you for reading and GOD bless you.**

ACKNOWLEDGEMENTS

I thank and praise GOD for inspiring me to write this book. I also thank and praise HIM for every single blessing in my life. It's my honor and pleasure to serve HIM, and I will do so for as long as I'm on this earth and beyond that.

Thank you to my wonderful and beautiful wife Linda. She's stuck by me through thick and thin, and I praise GOD for her. She is a good and decent woman of GOD, and I love her more than she knows.
Thank you to my family, friends and my clients. I love all of you! Special thank you to my dear friends Melinda Gagnon, along with Annette Munnich at Stellium Books.

TESTIMONIALS

All that I can say is Thank GOD for Bill Bean!!! I felt the weight of those attached demons lift from me as he commanded them to be gone. And just as suddenly, I felt the intensely profound infusion of GRACE OF THE HOLY SPIRIT enter into every fiber and cell of my body and mind!

Those demons, who by the way, left screeching and screaming as warrior angels carried them off into the night sky, had been attached to me most likely for the major part of my entire life from the early age of 2 to my current life as a mother and grandmother. When they fled, so did my lifelong struggle with anxiety, depression, suicide, and fear! All the demonic and paranormal activity fled as well.

While I understand that I was delivered through the GRACE OF GOD, working in Bill Bean, I am eternally in Bill's debt. He saved me and gave me a life. A life that I was always meant to have.

Melinda Gagnon
Assistant to Bill Bean

****

I first heard Bill Bean on the Coast to Coast radio show. That same night I sent him an email and he called me the next day. He helped deliver our church from the dark forces who had taken up residence in our old building. Bill has a GOD given gift for facing demonic and satanic forces. He stands against evil through powerful prayers and GOD answers his prayers of deliverance. Bill Bean is a force of GOD'S light and has become a great friend of mine. I know GOD can help deliver others from the hand of Satan through Bill Bean.

Pastor/Evangelist Jonathan Cobb
First Baptist Church West Harwich, MA

****

I was under demonic oppression and had attempted suicide several times. Then through a friend I was guided to Bill Bean. Since meeting Bill, my life has been totally transformed and I'm forever grateful to God for working through Bill to save my life. I feel that Bill Bean is one of God's mightiest warriors on this Earth!

Sgt. John Drenner

****

I was sick, depressed and dealing with something very dark in my life. Then I met Bill Bean and my life changed in a very short amount of time. I lost 123 pounds and regained my health after a decade of horrible sickness. God worked through Bill to give me a brand new life. I currently use my life experience along with Bill's teachings to help others. I have learned so much from Bill and consider him as my best friend.

Jeff Leeper

****

Your interview on Access Radio in the UK helped my lost boy to come back. I was having some problems with my 16 year old son, and I could see him drifting off the rails. So I got him to listen to your interview, and he heard you speak about your terrible childhood, how hard it was for you and how your family was destroyed. You also talked about having to quit school in the 8th grade and go to work. You mentioned that you made mistakes, but turned your life around. Then when you mentioned writing three books, and it inspired him. You have had such a positive impact on him, and now he's fixing his life and is determined to be the best that he can be. Thank you, Mr. Bean for your words and for inspiring my son to do better. It's made a big difference and for that, I'm truly grateful.

Helen Beachell

****

I have encountered many people in my life that have claimed to be healers and lightworkers, but you sir, are the only one I have ever known to be the "real deal" . You are not just a man of God, you are one of his mighty warriors!

Marcus Leader

****

Bill thank you very much for all of the help you have given to me and my family. You are truly a man of God and I wish you all the love of God in everything you do

Steven Wolfe

****

Bill, you are truly a gift from God. I was at the end of my rope, and I'm forever in your debt. If I can ever assist you in any way, I'm at your disposal. I am truly looking forward to moving on with my life, without the heavy chains of oppression. God Bless you. THANK YOU!

Sean Darby

****

Bill, I thank you so very much for coming to help me, and for using the gifts that God has anointed you with. I was in such horrible despair and was so hopeless. I was terribly depressed, and the pain I felt was unbearable. I prayed and ask the Lord to send someone to help me, and he sent you. My life is forever changed after God worked through you to deliver me from evil. I'm so overjoyed that I can't contain myself in my endless praise to God. Bill has the ability to make you feel comfortable and safe. I was able to speak freely and truthfully to him and it was amazing to feel all of the negativity lifting from me. I will forever consider Bill Bean to be family, and I love Bill Bean for coming all the way to Georgia to help me.

Sandra Clark

****

Hello Bill.
I heard you on the Kev Baker show on March 7th 2016, and my life will never be the same again.
Thank you for all you do.
God Bless you.

Daisy

48 years a hostage. For 48 years she was terrified of everything. People and darkness were the worst. You see, she wasn't always that way. It started when she was two years old. She remembers that night when the fear started. It started with seeing horrifying things in her room. Nothing earthly. They took glee is scaring her.

She saw these things in her room in the dead of the night. She screamed and cried, but was not believed. After several attempts of trying to tell someone (over the years growing up) she went silent. She isn't sure if the silence or disbelieving loved ones was worse.

In silence, she fell victim to the fear and endured it the best she could. Why did these evil things torment her all the time? Why wasn't she believed? She wanted to disappear at night and just exist when it was daylight.

She woke a few times to see "someone" looking into her eyes, almost nose to nose. She clearly remembered every detail. In an attempt to scream out for help, her voice was gone. She opened her mouth, but all that came out was silence.

The fear was " What are they gonna do to me if Mom isn't looking?" Cling to Mom and hide behind her was what she found worked. She was 5 years old and wanted nothing much to do with people. Finally, she moved to a place where it was just her family, no strangers. It was easier to not mingle if she didn't want to. Adults were not to be trusted and always feared, in her little mind. However, this did not stop the visitations of the evil that terrified her at night. She stopped telling anyone of the things she saw. She grew to know God and prayed and prayed every night for His help against these things. Still, it continued. Her heart beat so loud at times she believed someone should hear it in the stillness of the night. They would talk to her and say horrible things. They would wake her up and make her unable to move.

Telling her that her Bibles were not protecting her. You would think her story has a horrible ending, right? That she would give in and accept it all as a way of life, right? Think even having pastors tell her they either could not help or didn't believe it would discourage her, right? WRONG!!!!

Folks, don't believe the devil! He wants your life to be miserable and in bondage, be it by fear, hatred, bondage to someone or something in your life. You see, she found hope. After 48 years, yes, 48 YEARS of living this way, God heard her. He took up her case and freed her from the fear that literally controlled her. She NEVER went out at night. Kept sheets up over glass doors and windows. Could not be in a dark room at all (anxiety attack and would slither down the wall, sweating and heart racing). God set her free!!

If you guessed it by now, the person in the story was ME. A man by the name of Bill Bean (spiritual warrior/ deliverance minister of God) came when no one else would. He came armed with the Word of God and by the power of Almighty God. Bill did not only a deliverance on me but my home. By the power of God himself I was set free. Bill was willing to say yes to God to help me. That's saying so much. Pastors would not come here, Bill did. I am so grateful to God in Heaven for Bill being a willing vessel when the rest ran away because they didn't believe in it. Thank you so much dear Jesus in Heaven! We have an awesome God.

Since that night God delivered me, the lighting in my house has almost made me squint, it is so bright. I thought for years it was dim, not so! That fear that I saw with my eyes in the evil visitations was removed. Thank you brother Bill Bean. I love you and your wife both. God bless you and THANK YOU for being that willing vessel!

Chiryl Goodman Arnott

Bill Bean is one of the most sincere, amazing and extraordinary individuals I have ever had the good fortune to meet. His heartbreaking and terrifying story is unforgettable and his transformation into a man of such deep faith and devotion is a gift to us all. Bill works around the U.S. walking through doors to be the answer to whatever pain and evil lurk inside. For this reason, he has become one of my personal heroes.

Annette Munnich
Publisher/ Stellium Books

Pics by Patti Bean, Bob Sigmon (cover pic) and Bill Bean (Divine Pic)

THE CONNECTION

WILLIAM J. BEAN JR.

Bill Bean is a nationally known author and lecturer. He is an experiencer, victim, survivor, and conqueror of evil. His faith in GOD has inspired many people around the country and in different parts of the world. Bill says, "GOD truly delivered me from evil." William John Bean was born in Baltimore, Maryland. His parents were William and Patricia Bean. Bill has a sister named Patti and a brother named Bobby.

In his book Dark Force, Bill Bean painfully describes in terrifying detail the events that tormented his family. As disturbing as some of the content in Dark Force is, there's a very powerful message of hope and faith that has affected many readers in a positive way.

Bill starred in a Discovery Channel broadcast about his story. The show aired on September 7, 2006, on the series, "A Haunting." The segment is called "House of the Dead" and it remains one of the most watched segments. It's often shown during Bill's lectures, along with a jaw dropping photo presentation. Bill has taken many bizarre photos of anomalous phenomena over the years.

Bill Bean travels around the country leaving audiences both riveted and inspired. He has also given hundreds of interviews and is always in demand for lectures, conventions, and show appearances.

Bill says, "I truly know the awesome power of GOD and the vulgar power of Satan."

To Contact Bill: billbean104@yahoo.com
beanoffice@yahoo.com
http://www.billbean.net
Follow my blog thespiritualwarriorsite.wordpress.com

MORE BOOKS BY BILL BEAN

Dark Force: The Tragic Story of the Bean Family
Best Seller in Supernatural
Paperback and Kindle on Amazon
Stellium Books 2016

72416931R00075

Made in the USA
San Bernardino, CA
24 March 2018